For my mother and father,
for Dr. Ben,
and for Rebecca,
without whose loving care of my daughters
this book could never have been written

112015

Word People

by Nancy Caldwell Sorel
illustrated by Edward Sorel

AMERICAN HERITAGE PRESS   NEW YORK

Library of Congress Catalog Card Number: 71-117358
SBN-07-059648-4

CONTENTS

PREFACE

When we first conceived *Word People*, we anticipated that it would include some two to three dozen eponymous personalities. For a brief period we even wondered whether the idea would stretch to book length. When our collection had passed fifty without any lack of further candidates, it became clear that we would have to impose some limitations, and the following rules were devised:

1. The word must appear in the standard American dictionaries.
2. The word must appear uncapitalized.
3. The word must appear alone, with no second word following.
4. The word must apply to a specific object, condition, action, or type of action, rather than to a general philosophy or system of thought (as in platonic, Socratic, Machiavellian, sophistic).
5. The word must appear in more than one dictionary with the same etymological source.
6. Only the most commonly used scientific terms would be included.

We must confess to our exceptions. "Fahrenheit" and "Pullman" are capitalized; "teddy" is invariably followed by "bear"; and "napoleon" has nothing whatsoever to do with Napoleon. But the reader is spared the Mae West, the Sam Browne, the Dr. Denton, and Levis, as well as the Wellington boot, Eiffel tower, ferris wheel, melba toast, Colt revolver, bowie knife, Fallopian tube, and Caesarean section, to mention but a few.

With willing loyalty we have taken our definitions from *The American Heritage Dictionary of the English Language.*

Finally, we would never have collected our eighty-odd eponyms without the help of our friends. They brought us "word people" as visitors bring a bottle of wine; they consulted *their* friends, who consulted *their* friends; they woke us up with new ones they had thought (dreamed?) up during the night. Each time we believed that we had finished, a friend made yet another addition to our list. Thus we offer the following collection with much trepidation, hoping that future dictionaries will not include

sorelogy (sô-rĕl'ō-jē) *n.* An incomplete listing or guide.

Nancy Sorel
Edward Sorel

ampere (ăm′pîr′) *n.* A unit of electric current in the meter-kilogram-second system. It is the steady current that when flowing in straight parallel wires of infinite length and negligible cross section, separated by a distance of one meter in free space, produces a force between the wires of 2×10^{-7} newtons per meter of length. Also shortened to "amp."

ndré Marie Ampère was eighteen years old when his father was guillotined — a victim of the Reign of Terror in France. The sensitive young man thus lost not only a parent but the only teacher he had ever had, and the shock was so great that for well over a year he could neither speak nor read, but spent most of his time lying on his back staring at the sky. When he again took an interest in life, he returned to the study of algebra, in which he was already very advanced, and he began also to write poetry. When he was twenty-four, he married a beautiful young girl from a neighboring town and the next year accepted a professorship in a school at Bourg-en-Bresse. But a few years later his young wife died, and Ampère was again plunged into gloom.

This time, however, he sought relief in work. His

varied interests ranged from transcendental mathematics to animal physiology, from electricity and magnetism to psychology; he was fascinated by psychology and worked untiringly to establish it as a science. His most important discoveries, however, centered on electricity. He was the first to explain that the earth's magnetism is a result of terrestrial electric currents circulating from east to west around the globe. He established mathematically and demonstrated physically the law of the mechanical action between electric currents, which became the cardinal formula in electrodynamics and was accepted as one of the most brilliant achievements of science. He also invented the astatic needle and contributed to the invention of the electric telegraph by proposing the use of a number of circuits and magnetic needles, each of which would be identified with a letter of the alphabet.

It has been said of Ampère that he could not think while sitting down; sometimes he stood, more often he paced. Whether or not he was also a peripatetic chess player has not been passed down to us—just that the game was his great passion, that the board was always set up in the corner of his workroom, and that no visitor in a hurry was advised to enter there.

begonia (bĭ-gōn′yə) *n.* Any of various plants of the genus *Begonia,* mostly native to the tropics but widely cultivated, having leaves that are often brightly colored or veined and irregular, waxy flowers of various colors.

Born in the reign of Louis XIII, Michel Bégon held only minor government posts until his marriage to a cousin of Colbert's opened the way to his employment as a kind of assistant treasurer of the Navy at Toulon, Brest, and Le Havre. Although he was usually referred to as governor of Santo Domingo, it appears that he never actually held that post, but rather was sent there as commissioner to support the government's policy of protecting the natives from the less enlightened designs of the merchants. Bégon was particularly concerned with the religious and medical needs of the island. In all probability, he carried the begonia back to France with him and introduced it to the botanists of Europe.

Bégon went on to serve as administrator of the ports of Rochefort and la Rochelle. During the years he amassed a large library, which he opened to the public. When his librarian warned him that by so doing he was sure to lose several books, he replied: "I had much rather lose my books, than seem to distrust an honest man."

Amelia Jenks Bloomer

bloomer (bloo′mər) *n.* 1. A costume formerly worn by women and girls that was composed of loose trousers gathered about the ankles and worn under a short skirt. 2. *Plural.* Wide, loose trousers gathered at the knee and formerly worn by women and girls as an athletic costume.

Although she had persuaded her husband to omit the word "obey" from their marriage vows, Amelia Jenks Bloomer was no nineteenth-century Women's Liberationist. She would not sign the Declaration of Independence for Women that was drawn up right in her own town of Seneca Falls, New York, and her real concern was temperance, not feminism. She contributed articles (signed "Gloriana" or "Eugene") on morality, alcoholism, and other social issues to the *Free Soil Union* and the *Seneca County Courier,* but her enterprising spirit was not satisfied, and she resolved to start her own magazine.

The Lily was officially the house organ of the Seneca Falls Ladies' Temperance Society, but to all intents and purposes it was the personal mouthpiece for the crusading opinions of its petite and rather pretty editor. "A simple young thing with no experience, no education for business, in no way fitted for such work," Amelia Bloomer described herself to a subscriber. Nevertheless, she established her pressroom in the room adjoining the post office (she was also deputy postmaster), wrote copy, read proof, edited, contracted for the printing, and by herself wrapped and mailed all the copies that her public had subscribed to at fifty cents a year. It was the first women's magazine in America.

In spite of these innovations, Mrs. Bloomer's neighbors were hardly prepared for her sudden appearance on the town's main thoroughfare with her skirt apparently shrunk all the way up to her knees and the lower half of her legs enveloped in a kind of Turkish trouser. In truth, credit for inventing this scandalous attire must go to the wealthy abolitionist Gerrit Smith, whose fashionable daughter, Mrs. Elizabeth Smith Miller, first wore it. Amelia Bloomer was merely joining the reaction against the voluminous hoopskirts that fashion decreed for every lady. The hoops could be propelled through doorways only with difficulty, and they were especially ill-suited to the unpaved streets of small-town America. After *The Lily* took up the cause of dress reform and even included patterns for the new costume, Gerrit Smith's invention became permanently associated with the name of the magazine's editor.

Mrs. Bloomer and her disciples were soon swept up in a tremendous hubbub, for the new fashion was as feverishly discussed as the Fugitive Slave Law or abolition. A large Boston daily wrote glowingly in its society section of a bride attired "in the poetry and bloom of a Bloomer costume . . . of elegant white satin," and the Brooklyn *Eagle* raved about "a young lady, apparently in the bloom of her teens, and beautiful as a bouquet of roses . . . her limbs, which appeared symmetrical as the chiseled pedestals of a sculptured Venus, encased in a pair of yellow pantaloons." But *Godey's Lady's Book* disapproved, and Gordon Bennett's New York *Herald* was vehemently opposed: ". . . the attempt to introduce pantaloons . . . will not succeed. Those who have tried it, will very likely soon end their career in the lunatic asylum, or, perchance, in the State prison."

The raging battle produced side skirmishes hardly less interesting. A certain reverend of Easthampton, Massachusetts, forbade two Bloomer girls to enter his church, threatening them with excommunication and causing periodicals on both sides of the issue to temporarily unite in denouncing him for such an unwarranted assumption of holy authority. Another and more famous divine, Dr. DeWitt Talmage, cited Moses as an early opponent of Bloomerism ("A woman shall not wear anything that pertains to a man . . ." Deuteronomy 22:5), but Mrs. Bloomer countered with Genesis, which, she pointed out, makes no distinction between the fig leaves of Adam and Eve.

The fashion crossed the Atlantic when a small band of proselytizing Bloomer girls invaded England. A "London Bloomer Committee" was formed and almost immediately issued a handbill announcing that "a public lecture relating to the same will be delivered at the Royal Soho Theatre on Oct. 6. The ladies of the committee will themselves appear in full Bloomer costume, and the mothers and daughters of England are cordially invited to attend." Such lectures began to crop up all over England, and although they were generally accompanied by considerable hissing and laughter, they were sufficiently threatening to the conservative mind to stimulate "Anti-Bloomer Addresses." That winter "A Grand Bloomer Ball" was held in the elegant Hanover Square Rooms, and although it was attended by youthful members of both Houses of Parliament as well as Guards, officers, dandies, writers, painters, actors, and barristers (among others), too few of the bloomer-clad ladies present were exactly "respectable," and the bloomer lost face accordingly. "I went yesterday . . . to see . . . a group of Bloomers in Madame Tussaud's Show," the Duke of Wellington wrote to Lady Salisbury in 1851. "It is impossible that the Costume should be adopted."

The Duke proved to be right. The general mockery that first greeted the bloomer never abated, and although the feminists continued to wear the bloomer for a few years, even they gave it up in time. Feeling martyred in Seneca Falls, Amelia and her husband moved west, where the fame (but not the ridicule) had preceded her. They settled happily in Council Bluffs, Iowa, where Mrs. Bloomer continued to wear the costume for a few more years. She gave it up when the Union cause superseded feminism and dress reform in her heart. The guns at Fort Sumter were hardly silent before she had organized the Soldiers' Aid Society; it met in her home to stitch the large silk flag which Company B of the Fourth Iowa Volunteer Infantry eventually received from her hands. "You are now going forth to sustain and defend the Constitution," emoted Mrs. Bloomer at the presentation, "against an unjust and monstrous rebellion, fomented and carried on by wicked and ambitious men who have for their object the overthrow of the best government the world has ever seen." A local reporter, recording the scene, noted that among the volunteers "many a brawny breast heaved, and tears trickled down many a manly face." Amelia Bloomer had won them at last!

Sir Robert Peel

bobby (bŏb′ē) *n. British Slang.* A policeman.

Because the English bobby's *raison d'être* is to keep the peace, it is most appropriate that he should have been named for Sir Robert Peel. Not that Sir Robert ever walked a beat—far from it, for he was trained from the cradle to become Prime Minister much as the Prince of Wales is trained to become king. But Peel's philosophy mirrored that of each bobby: never instigate, never create, never envision; direct all your energy toward maintaining the status quo and accept change only when it has become obvious to everyone that you cannot keep the peace any other way. Yet Sir Robert Peel probably had a greater impact than any other man on the English political scene during the first half of the nineteenth century.

Peel's life may have been quite exciting, for English politics are rarely dull, and Sir Robert had a disconcerting habit of changing sides at the last moment. But his is not a dramatic life in retrospect, for all those bills are no longer hanging fire—Catholic Emancipation is an established fact; the Reform Bill has long since been accepted by the Lords, and the

Corn Laws (the greatest fight of them all) have been repealed. Because all this is known history instead of daily drama, there is little else to say about the life of Sir Robert Peel. He was a strange political animal — an M.P. incarnate. At home there was a loyal (if perhaps not overly clever) wife and children, who were surely a great pride and comfort to him, but one hears little of them and equally little of any other diversions. Byron, who was in the same form with Peel at Harrow, wrote: "As a scholar, he was greatly my superior; as a declaimer and actor, I was reckoned at least his equal; as a schoolboy out of school, I was always in scrapes — he never." School became Parliament, but nothing else changed.

In English politics before the reforms of 1832, one could lose one's parliamentary seat in an open election one day and buy another with hard cash the next. This was not corruption; it was the system. There was nearly always a seat being offered on the open market, so that a rich politician never needed to fear being out of a job. The Peels were really quite rich; the moment that young Robert came of age, his father purchased a seat for him, and his career was launched.

Peel soon became Secretary for Ireland. The Irish were restless and were pressing hard for more rights. But Peel was much opposed to any enlargement of civil liberties. Who knew where it might end? Give them a political foot in the door and next thing they'd be wanting a religious foot too. They might even want to re-establish their own church in place of the established Protestant one. Such anti-Catholic sentiment soon earned him the nickname "Orange Peel," after the ultra-Protestant "orangemen" of Ireland. He was glad to leave Ireland when the time came — not, one has the feeling, because he was bothered by the injustice of the British system there, or by the poverty and hunger of the general populace, but rather because his sterling qualities of diligence and decorum were not ones that appealed to the Irish imagination.

At Westminster, however, these qualities were much in demand. Peel became Home Secretary and promptly created the Metropolitan Police Force (in Ireland he had established the Royal Irish Constabulary). Denounced in street bills as "Peel's Bloody Gang" — later shortened to "peelers" and "bobbies" — the M.P.F. was of much initial concern to a worried populace, who viewed it as a body created specially to suppress their legitimate discontent. Peel managed to institute many reforms in criminal law that had been advocated unsuccessfully by others for years, including the abolition of the death penalty for petty offenses. (It was retained only for murder, treason, and forging a Bank of England note.) But here again change was a necessity, for with the punishment so far outweighing the crime, common juries were refusing to convict, and many offenders were escaping punishment entirely. Peel was far from being opposed to capital punishment *per se,* as evidenced by letters to him from George IV begging him not to hang quite so many condemned prisoners.

It would be unfair to consider Peel merely a politician of expediency, but certainly he did not seem to hold his beliefs very strongly. Perhaps it was fortunate that he did not, for he was a very strong force in his party, and every time he reversed himself on an issue, political liberties in England were advanced. After his vociferous support of the anti-Catholic cause, he came to agree with Wellington that Catholics must, after all, be given the right to sit in Parliament. Thus he not only voted for, but actually introduced the Catholic Emancipation Bill, which then passed. During the long debate on the Reform Bill, however, Peel remained cautiously in the background—Wellington could afford to lead the opposition; he had already been Prime Minister.

When Peel himself became Prime Minister for the first time, he lasted exactly one hundred days, but six years later he returned to that position and held it for five years. The country was in severe economic straits. Peel abolished many customs duties and instituted the income tax, temporarily so he thought. When the Commons passed a Mining Act stipulating that only children over ten could be employed in the mines, Peel insisted that the decision be reversed or he would resign. He was convinced that English trade would suffer without a supply of cheap child labor. Finally, however, faced with a starving population in Ireland and an only slightly less hungry working class at home, he was forced to advocate the repeal of the Corn Laws, which by withdrawing the protective tariff on imported grain brought about one of the most vital changes in English history.

On June 29, 1850, Sir Robert Peel was thrown from his horse. Three days later he was dead.

bowdlerize (bōd′lə-rīz, boud′–) *tr.v.* To expurgate prudishly.

Thomas Bowdler was one of those lucky people who should have been born exactly when they were. He was as much a product of the nineteenth century as the nineteenth century was a product of him. Long before Victoria succeeded to the throne, Bowdler was hacking away at Shakespeare—rendering his plays fit for the chaste and religious, gouging out all those unhappy expressions which, as he says in the preface to the second edition of his *Family Shakespeare,* "however they might be tolerated in the sixteenth century, are by no means admissible in the nineteenth. . . ."

Bowdler was a member of a Shropshire family that abounded in prolific writers of letters and sermons. Each male Bowdler was named Thomas or John, alternately. The Thomas with whom we are concerned studied medicine at his father's wish, and after his graduation from Edinburgh took the Grand Tour. It was evidently an eye-opening experience, and Thomas returned to his native land blessing God for having made him an Englishman.

Thomas Bowdler

Young Dr. Bowdler settled down to practice medicine in London, but (alas!) he very soon discovered himself unfit for his life's work. The sight of anyone in pain drove him nearly to distraction. Happily, his father died just about then, leaving his son quite comfortably off well before he was thirty.

Thomas' debut with the pen was the publication of a series of letters he had written from Holland during the Tour. His style, as was perhaps natural in a neophyte, was hesitant—he set down nothing that he had not verified, except for a very few reliable rumors. And even then he was careful to note just how reliable the rumor was and to disclaim responsibility for its veracity. On the very eve of the Revolution he traveled to France, but the only recorded results of that trip were his joining the Proclamation Society and the "Society for the Suppression of Vice," both organizations formed for the purpose of combating immoral influences emanating from Paris.

In 1800 Bowdler apparently renounced society and retired to the Isle of Wight where he lived in modified seclusion for ten years. It was probably during this period that he became concerned lest England's young ladies grow old without having read Shakespeare's plays. These could not, of course, be read as they stood, for they were far too indelicate. This, then, would be Bowdler's life's work, his *magnum opus* —to render Shakespeare fit to be read aloud by a gentleman in the company of ladies. In 1818 Bowdler's first edition of the ten-volume *Family Shakespeare* appeared. Rosalind and Celia had become polite, cultivated young ladies, Hamlet spoke with restrained decorum to Ophelia, Falstaff was a different man, and Doll Tearsheet was excised.

That there should be criticism of his efforts never ceased to surprise Bowdler. He preferred to think that Shakespeare, in his heart of hearts, regretted such lapses in his writings, and would have been grateful to him, Bowdler, for purging them. Replying to his critics, he wrote: "And shall I be classed with the Assassins of Caesar, because I have rendered these invaluable plays fit for the perusal of our virtuous females? IF ANY WORD OR EXPRESSION IS OF SUCH A NATURE, THAT THE FIRST IMPRESSION WHICH IT EXCITES IS AN IMPRESSION OF OBSCENITY, THAT WORD OUGHT NOT TO BE SPOKEN, OR WRITTEN, OR PRINTED, AND IF PRINTED, OUGHT TO BE ERASED."

Shakespeare salvaged, Bowdler turned his scalpel to Gibbon, and before long issued a new *Decline and Fall.* Anticipating a renewal of criticism, Bowdler concluded his introduction with "my firm and sincere belief that if it were possible for the celebrated historian to deliver his sentiments at the present moment, he would say that he desired nothing more ardently than the laying aside the former editions of his history and trusting his fame and reputation to . . . the present publication."

It is perhaps fortunate for Chaucer, Donne, and other masters of the English language that in 1825, at the age of seventy-one, Bowdler died of a cold, caught, as he wrote shortly before his death, "at Swansea whilst transacting some distressing business."

boycott (boi′kŏt′) *tr. v.* To abstain from using, buying, or dealing with, as a protest or means of coercion. —*n.* The act or an instance of boycotting.

Captain Charles C. Boycott did not invent, propose, or practice the policy that bears his name. An impulsive but dignified, almost austere Englishman, he would surely have lived and died in obscurity had not his life—to his own misfortune—crossed that of the great Irish nationalist leader Charles Parnell. Boycotting, at that time a nameless political tactic, was one of Parnell's foremost weapons in the battle for Irish independence, and Captain Boycott was its first victim.

Charles Cunningham Boycott had been trained as a soldier but had resigned his commission on his marriage and had gone with his wife to farm a wild estate on Achill Island off the western coast of Ireland. Though reasonably successful in their endeavor, the Boycotts soon returned to the mainland so that the captain could accept an appointment as the Earl of Erne's agent on the earl's estates at Connaught in County Mayo.

Ireland in the 1870's was an unhappy country of poverty-stricken peasants governed by absentee land-

lords. Yet an increasingly restive and articulate na-
tionalistic feeling among the people was crystalizing
into the Home Rule movement. Land was the crucial
issue, and the people had long been united in demanding the "three F's"—fair rent, fixity of tenure,
and freedom of sale. Under the Land Act of 1870,
the tenant could become proprietor of his land, but
when Boycott first came to County Mayo three years
later, he found the countryside in the grip of an
agricultural depression, which was to continue for
the next two decades.

In 1880 agrarian agitation took a new turn. Charles
Parnell, Member of Parliament and President of the
Irish National Land League, had just returned from
the United States, where, as the darling of Irish-
Americans from Boston to Baltimore, he had raised
£70,000 for the Irish cause. Determined to take the
initiative, Parnell decided on a new tactic: ostracism.
Either the tenant or the landlord might be ostracized
—the tenant if he attempted to buy land from which
another tenant had been evicted; the landlord if he
failed to accept a reduced rent fixed by the tenants
themselves.

"Now what are you to do to a tenant who bids for
a farm from which his neighbor has been evicted?"
asked Parnell of his wildly cheering supporters in a
town near Connaught on September 19, 1880. "You
must show him on the roadside when you meet him,
you must show him in the streets of the town, you
must show him at the shop counter, you must show
him in the fair and in the marketplace, and even in
the house of worship, by leaving him severely alone!"

Thus it was that Lord Erne's estates, so conveniently close by, were selected as a test case. His tenants got together and fixed a new rent well below what Erne had prescribed, then offered their terms to Boycott. Now the Captain's position was clear: he could not, as an agent, do anything other than uphold his employer's legal rights. He therefore refused the reduction. The tenants stood their ground, and Boycott promptly sat down and wrote out ejectments against them.

Just three days after Parnell's speech, a process-server attempting to deliver the ejectments was stopped by a band of hostile peasants before he reached the first tenant's cottage. He was forced to retreat precipitately to the captain. The next day the peasants advanced to Boycott's house and ordered all the servants to leave, which they promptly did. Within a few hours, Captain Boycott's neat, orderly world had become a nightmare. Suddenly there were no farm laborers to gather the harvest, no stablemen to care for the horses, no cook to prepare dinner nor maid to serve it. The local shopkeepers were forbidden to serve Boycott when he entered their stores; the blacksmith was not to shoe his horse nor the laundress to wash his clothes, and even the post-boy was warned against carrying Boycott's letters. "You must show him," Charles Parnell had said, "by leaving him severely alone!"

In the end, it took no less than fifty men imported from Ulster and guarded by British soldiers to harvest Lord Erne's crops on the shores of Lough Mask. As the pressure increased, Captain Boycott and his wife were forced to seek refuge for some time in a barn, where at considerable personal risk they were suc- cored by friends from the village. The following year the Boycotts left Ireland. Parnell was the victor in more ways than one, for in 1881 the "Magna Carta" of the Irish farmer was passed. This Land Act recog- nized the "three F's" and set up a land commission to fix a "fair rent."

One might assume that Charles Boycott would have shunned Ireland forever after, but that was not the case. He revisited it some years later while on holiday, was recognized at a public gathering in Dublin, and was generously cheered; the Irish attributed his former behavior to his army-trained sense of duty and bore him no grudge.

braille (brāl) *n.* A system of writing and printing for the blind, in which varied arrangements of raised dots representing letters and numerals can be identified by touch.

Louis Braille was the son of a harness maker of the village of Coupvray outside Paris. At the age of three, while playing in his father's workshop, he drove an awl into his left eye, and in the course of a few weeks went blind in both eyes. Napoleon's reforms had not extended to the weak or handicapped, and a blind child was usually either trained as a professional beggar or set to shoveling coal in a factory. Simon René Braille, however, was determined that his son should suffer no such fate. Louis attended the village school until he was ten. Then his father drove him to Paris and entered him in the Institution Nationale des Jeunes Aveugles.

The Institution had in its library at that time exactly three books, each of which was divided into twenty parts weighing some twenty pounds each. The contents of these volumes were engraved in large embossed letters, and from these Louis learned to read. He was an exceptionally able student, both in his academic work and at the piano and organ, and before very long he was helping to teach the younger children.

In the same year that Louis Braille entered the Institution, a certain Charles Barbier, an artillery captain in Louis XVIII's army, reported to the Academy of Sciences on his invention of "night writing"—a system of dots and dashes in relief on thin cardboard by which sentinels, using predetermined combinations, could send messages to each other at night. When Barbier later brought his work to the Institution, young Braille set about to improve it. Working silently in bed at night with his board, stylus, and reams of soft paper, he tried and discarded this method and that until finally he hit upon a system of writing using only dots. He discovered that a simple key pattern of two dots across and three dots down—six all together—had quite a number of possible variations. Using this pattern as his "cell," Braille gradually devised sixty-three separate combinations representing all the letters in the French alphabet (w was added later at the request of an Englishman), accents, punctuation marks, and mathematical signs.

Dr. Pignier, director of the Institution and Braille's sympathetic supporter, adopted his method almost immediately, and for a few happy years Braille saw his system flourish there while he himself taught, attended courses at the Collège de France, served as organist at Notre Dame des Champs, and by applying his system to musical notation, began to compose. His musical talents were immediately recognized; he gave a concert that was acclaimed by many of the foremost musicians of his day and he began to frequent the many musical salons of the French capital.

But government bureaucracy prevented his system from being officially adopted at the Institution, and when Pignier left, his successor insisted that the teachers return to the officially approved embossed letters. Braille's method went underground: the students continued to learn and use it, but surreptitiously, and they were punished if caught.

There exists a very romantic story of how the French government finally realized the superiority of the Braille method over all other reading systems for the blind. Supposedly, a lovely, young, and very talented blind girl, Thérèse von Kleinert, to whom Braille had taught the organ and his reading method, performed at the fashionable salon of a wealthy Parisian lady before many of the intellectuals of the day. After the applause, she informed her audience that the person they should be honoring was a man named Louis Braille, who had developed the system that enabled her to copy out her many musical scores and to read and write. She noted sadly that Braille was dying of tuberculosis unheralded and unrecognized. According to the story, Thérèse's disclosure turned the tables, and Braille's system was very soon adopted all over France.

Henry Brougham

brougham (brōōm) *n.* 1. A closed four-wheeled carriage with an open driver's seat in front. 2. An automobile with an open driver's seat. 3. An electrically powered automobile resembling a coupé.

There goes Solon, Lycurgus, Demosthenes, Archimedes, Sir Isaac Newton, Lord Chesterfield, and a great many more in one post-chaise," remarked the nineteenth century English poet and conversationalist Samuel Rogers of his friend Henry Brougham. Brougham was a man of great energy and versatility —a scientist, writer, lawyer, politician, reformer, critic, mathematician. Even the little closed carriage that he designed practically revolutionized the carriage-building business.

Henry Brougham was born in Edinburgh in the middle of George III's reign. He was a tall, gawky, homely boy with a long bobbling nose that was in time to become the cartoonist's delight. Mathematics was his first interest (by the time he was twenty, three of his papers had been published by the Royal Society), but his fondness for talking persuaded him to study law. However, he was too fond of airing his liberal opinions to practice law successfully in Scotland, so he and his friends started the *Edinburgh Review*; at twenty-three, he was its most prolific contributor.

Two years later, in 1804, Brougham moved to London, and it was as though he had found his natural habitat. The Whig Party opened its arms to him—he had no social standing and no money, but he was *so* brilliant, witty, and charming. He was elected to both the Royal Society and the King of Clubs, the latter of whose members were supposed to be the thirty cleverest men in London. Brougham soon knew everyone worth knowing and, seemingly, everyone knew him. In a few years he became a force to be reckoned with; so much so that when he was called to the bar at the age of thirty, the Tories sent both the Attorney-General and the Solicitor-General to vote against him.

But Brougham's popularity was not universal, even among the Whigs. The more cautious and aristocratic of them found him too revolutionary. However, once he entered Parliament, he quickly became the leading force in his party. In eloquent, fighting speeches he opposed the status quo with the same fervor (and considerably more brilliance) that Peel (who entered the Commons at the same time—see *bobby*) employed to uphold it. His rise at the bar was spectacular; he was the advocate for anyone and everyone who found himself in conflict with the oppressive Tory system. Jeremy Bentham, William Wilberforce, Henry Thornton, Zachary Macaulay were all his friends.

Brougham took up many causes—the slave trade, the lack of education for the working classes, the inhumanity of both the civil and criminal law codes, the savage floggings suffered by soldiers and sailors for misdemeanors, censorship of the press. And then there was Queen Caroline. How Brougham happened to take up her cause is uncertain, except that he loathed her husband, the regent (later King George IV). The marriage had never been even tolerable. Caroline was forcibly separated from their daughter, the Princess Charlotte, and excluded from court life—which was more than enough to gain her the sympathy of the average Britisher. Finally Caroline abandoned England, went abroad, and there threw caution to the winds. Her clothes, her parties, her travel, and most of all her association with her Italian courier Bergami became the scandal of the Continent. Her husband, not at all displeased, bided his time, then sent a commission to Milan to inquire into her conduct. When mad George III finally died and his son, the regent, at last succeeded to the throne, Caroline was offered £50,000 to renounce her title as queen and remain abroad. She refused and left on a ship for Dover, where she was welcomed by a deliriously enthusiastic mob.

The king countered by requesting his ministers to introduce a Bill of Divorce into the House of Lords. The bill, which was in all respects degrading to the queen, would annul the marriage because of her adultery with Bergami. The prosecution produced a string of Italian witnesses whom Brougham, as Caroline's advocate, set out to discredit: this witness was paid such-and-such an amount; that witness was in collusion with another—the poor Italians incurred the fury of practically the entire English populace and more than once had to be saved from mobs. The odds against Brougham had seemed overwhelming, and his brilliant defense was declared a model of eloquence. The aristocracy was visibly shaken, and the bill was withdrawn. But the king had the last move. Caroline arrived at the doors of Westminster Abbey for his coronation only to find them barred against her.

Yet Brougham was more than the acknowledged defender of oppressed innocence. He also inaugurated the Society for the Diffusion of Useful Knowledge and founded London University, with its liberal enrollment policies. He was elected M.P. from Yorkshire, which was by far the most important county constituency in England. But after he had succeeded in toppling the Duke of Wellington's government and bringing the Whigs into power, he found himself excluded from the cabinet by order of the king himself (now William IV). Because he was clearly the most powerful and popular Whig, Brougham was finally persuaded, for the sake of the party, to accept the Chancellorship, become a peer, and move from the Commons to the Lords. On the day he took his seat on the woolsack, the official seat of the Lord Chancellor in the House of Lords, the gallery and court were packed with spectators, including princes, dukes, and foreign ambassadors. As chancellor he was much renowned: "People came to town to see the Tower, the lions, and Brougham in the Court of Chancery," wrote one contemporary.

But Brougham was never a very good peer. His debating style was said to "lower the tone" of the Lords. His speech on the Reform Bill, however, was something else again, surpassing even his defense of Queen Caroline. For some three and a half hours on the last night of the debate, Brougham spoke before a House packed to suffocation. He was sustained through the session by frequent draughts of mulled port, and at the end, when he went down on his knees to implore the Lords not to vote against the bill, the port went to his head and he was unable to rise — or at least so thought his friends who picked him up and set him back on the woolsack. But the Lords were not to be moved so easily. They rejected the bill. Brougham had had difficulty for a long time in maintaining the balance between his tremendous natural abilities and his unstable and temperamental mind. After the defeat of the Reform Bill he became irascible and eccentric in the extreme. The king's mental condition was none too good, and it was reported that "his chancellor is not a little mad also."

The upshot was that Brougham finally meddled once too often in affairs that did not concern him and brought down the government. Although he never again held office, his political influence remained. When after a prolonged absence he returned to the Lords, he was greeted with an ovation by the peers, who had found their debates quite dull in his absence.

In the last quarter-century of his life (he lived to be ninety), he was much beloved for his eccentricities. He took up spiritualism and would hold conversations with the spirit of the Duke of Kent. He wore his favorite checked trousers (which were almost as much his trademark as his nose) everywhere, and drove about with Disraeli and Gladstone in that "garden chair on wheels," the original brougham. He had built a house in Cannes, was as quickly recognized in Paris as in London, and after the revolution of 1848 and the formation of the new Assembly, he was invited by the French to stand for the Department of Var. He was much pleased with the idea until he discovered that in acquiring French citizenship he would no longer have the right to call himself an Englishman. *Punch*, which had delighted in "doing him" ever since it began publication (its cover still depicts a little imp dragging the mask of Brougham behind him) reprinted its famous cartoon of "Brougham as a Citizen of the World" over the copy:

> Brougham a Frenchman? No, no, no; a million times no . . . Great Britain would fancy herself reduced in circumstances indeed if she were compelled to put down her BROUGHAM. . . . It is true that BROUGHAM has been at times somewhat crazy, and indeed, as some may have thought, rather shaky about the pole; but the BROUGHAM has been very serviceable in the long run, and we are disinclined to part with the old familiar article.

burke (bûrk) *tr.v.* 1. To murder (someone) by suffocation so as to leave the body intact and suitable for dissection. 2. To suppress quietly and unceremoniously.

When new discoveries in anatomy at the beginning of the nineteenth century made that subject more popular than ever among medical students, the University of Edinburgh School of Medicine, the most renowned in Europe, found its supply of cadavers insufficient to meet the demand. When lawful channels had been exhausted, the authorities were obliged to depend on body snatchers—persons who on dark nights dug up bodies from new graves to sell to the medical schools for dissection. It was a precarious business, and the corpses brought good prices, as William Burke and William Hare discovered when they offered for sale to a Dr. Knox in Surgeon's Square the body of an old pensioner who had died of natural causes in Hare's rooming house.

William Burke was an Irishman who had immigrated to Scotland, worked for some time on the Union Canal, and eventually drifted to Edinburgh. There he took up with a certain Helen McDougal and moved with her to the lodging house kept by Hare and his wife in Tanner's Close. Burke made an honest but meager living operating a kind of second-hand clothing business that specialized in the repair of old shoes, and he was no doubt tempted by the prospective profits of the body-marketing business. Thus when another of Hare's elder boarders became ill, the two men waited impatiently for his demise. When it looked as though he might recover, their disappointment was too much to bear. Burke found that it took only a moment to hold a pillow over the face of the luckless invalid, and then there it was — another £10 from Dr. Knox!

Whole new vistas opened up before the two men. Edinburgh was full of the old and friendless who would not be missed if they should suddenly disappear. Abagail Simpson, for example, an old beggar woman who had walked from her home in Gilmerton to Edinburgh to collect her pension — who was the wiser when she got drunk and just never walked back again? Two more old ladies followed her in quick succession, and Burke and Hare found themselves warming to their new profession. But when no stray indigents appeared for some days, Burke and Hare resorted to eighteen-year-old Mary Paterson for their fifth victim. It was a rash move on their part, for Mary's casual way of life had made her well-known among the young medical students themselves, not a few of whom recognized her voluptuous corpse. "Students crowded around the table on which she lay," wrote one of the young doctors, "and artists came to study a model worthy of Phidias and the best Greek art." Indeed, she was not even dissected immediately, but was put up in preservative as an example of the muscular development of the female form.

Effie, an old cinder gatherer, came next, followed in due course by a drunk woman whom Burke rescued from jail, a grandmother and her deaf and dumb grandson, and Anne McDougal, a cousin of Helen's whom they had invited to Edinburgh precisely because they needed another corpse. In her wake came a charwoman named Mrs. Hostler, followed by Mary Haldane and her daughter, both prostitutes. Burke and Hare laid themselves wide open to detection with the murder of "daft Jamie" — a simple-minded boy who had long been a great favorite of the students in Surgeons' Square, but it remained for their next victim to provide their undoing. Various stories exist as to how they were actually caught with the body of Mary Docherty, but caught they were, and all four — Burke, Helen McDougal, Hare, and his wife — were arrested and confined in Calton Hill Prison.

Hare, who was almost surely the brains behind the operation, denied all knowledge of any but the final murder of Mary Docherty and decided to give state's evidence. He and his wife eventually went free. The trial of Burke and Helen McDougal opened on Christmas Eve, and the jury went out at 8:30 on Christmas morning. They found Burke guilty on all counts, but they declared the case against Helen "not proven." The Lord Justice Clerk's sentence of death went on at great length, during which time the spectators cracked nuts, and two of the judges dozed peacefully.

Reports as to the actual number of victims varied from sixteen to thirty; even the lesser number inspired horror in the populace. But the joy with which the crowd outside the courtroom received the verdict was nothing compared to the exuberance with which they hanged Burke a month later. He had some distance to walk from the prison to the gallows erected in the Grassmarket, and the crowd, which had passed the night in eating, drinking, and general revelry, loaded him with curses. "Burke him!" shouted a voice, and then everywhere voices took up the cry, "Burke him! Burke him!" The authorities had all they could do to hang him before the mob broke loose.

After the event, Burke's body was taken from the jail to the college, where at one o'clock that afternoon a certain Professor Munro publicly dissected it and lectured for two hours on the deceased's brain. The following day a grand public exhibition was held: the dissected body was displayed on the black marble slab of the anatomical theater and some thirty thousand curious visitors filed past. The remains were then even more completely dissected, salted, and stored in appropriate barrels for use in future lectures at Surgeons' Square.

camellia (kə-mēl′yə) *n.* Any of several shrubs or trees of the genus *Camellia,* native to Asia; especially, *C. japonica,* having shiny evergreen leaves and showy, variously colored flowers.

Georg Josef Kamel, or Camel, was a Moravian Jesuit who went to the Philippines as a missionary late in the seventeenth century. He planted his herb garden in the grounds of the Jesuit college in Manila and used its annual harvest to supply the little pharmacy that he opened for the poor. The studies of the plants and natural history of the Philippines that he sent back to London were published in the *Philosophical Transactions* of the Royal Society of London. Carolus Linnaeus, who classified such things, named the camellia after him.

Earl of Cardigan

cardigan (kär′dĭ-gən) *n.* A sweater or knitted jacket opening down the front.

From his early childhood onward James Thomas Brudenell, later the Earl of Cardigan, wanted only to be a soldier. But he was the sole male heir to the family title and fortune, the adored brother of his seven sisters, and his family held his life too dear to allow him to risk it in the military. Perhaps because of this frustration his disposition soured. Although he was handsome, wealthy, and appeared to have the world at his feet, he became extremely harsh and domineering. His childhood fits of unreasonable rage continued throughout his life and finally played their part in the fate of six hundred British cavalrymen at the Battle of Balaclava.

By the time he was twenty-seven, it was obvious that James Brudenell was unfit for any profession other than the military. A parental compromise was reached, and because he was a member of the hereditary aristocracy, Brudenell took command of the 15th Hussars in 1824. He had a very high opinion of his military capabilities, and luckily for his ego, thirty years of peace stretched ahead. This was no reason for laxity on his part, however. Since merit was to be so long untried, appearance was of the utmost importance, and James Brudenell immediately ordered new uniforms for his troops, replaced English food with French food at their mess, and drilled them to a precision and swiftness of movement never before observed on the parade ground. The men were not used to such discipline in peacetime, but each infraction was taken as a personal affront by their fanatical commanding officer. Brudenell was convinced that even the horses were out to thwart him when they got sore backs. Had he not positively ordered that the horses were *not* to get sore backs? His continual rages and irrational acts kept him much in the public eye, and he was finally removed from his command after an officer whom he had illegally put under arrest was acquitted.

But James Brudenell without a regiment to command was like a child whose favorite toy has been taken from him, and to retrieve that toy became his obsession. Thus, no one who knew him was surprised when two years later, in spite of much Parliamentary opposition, he purchased for £40,000 the lieutenant colonelcy of the 11th Light Dragoons. What the 15th had at last escaped now descended upon the 11th, for the new commander saw only slackness and poor discipline around him. There were rules for everything; almost any offense was punishable; and while the regiment was quartered at Canterbury, the town jail was so filled with soldiers of the 11th that it became known as their regimental barracks. But, under Brudenell's command, they too were drilled to a new standard of perfection, and probably for that reason they were chosen in 1840 to meet Prince Albert on his arrival at Dover and to escort him to London for his marriage to Queen Victoria. Lord Cardigan—for James Brudenell had by now succeeded his father—was in his element. New uniforms were especially designed: cherry-colored trousers topped by jackets of royal blue edged with gold, furred pelisses, capes that glittered with braid and gold lace, and high fur hats with brilliant plumes.

Lord Cardigan was not one to learn from experience, and the difficulties he had encountered with the officers of the 15th were multiplied with the officers of the 11th. Several courts-martial were decided, quite unjustly, in Lord Cardigan's favor, which stimulated public indignation. He had to have police protection when he took a train to London, and once there he could not go to the theater without being confronted by a hissing crowd, yelling and shaking fists. When he attended a promenade concert the continuous uproar drowned out every note of music. The public was further incensed when he was acquitted by his peers of the charge of "firing a pistol with intent to murder" in a duel with one of his officers. (The trial was the first held in Westminster Hall since the Duchess of Kent had been tried for bigamy there.) Finally, Lord Cardigan had a soldier flogged before the entire regiment on Easter Sunday in the very building which had just been used for divine service. After that he had to drive around London in a closed carriage with the blinds pulled down.

Still, life within the regiment continued much as

before. The 11th was sent to Dublin, and a general pattern was duly established: an officer who broke some minor rule would be arrested by Cardigan, would appeal to the general, would be released and returned to his post. The officers seem to have spent much of their leisure writing letters of complaint to the general, and ultimately to the Duke of Wellington himself, who more than once was forced to intervene personally.

When the Crimean War broke out, Lord Cardigan applied at once for active duty to Lord Raglan (see *raglan*), Commander-in-Chief of the Expeditionary Force. Although Cardigan was fifty-six and had never seen active service, he was promoted to brigadier-general in command of the Light Brigade of Cavalry. Unfortunately, his immediate superior officer was his despised brother-in-law, Lord Lucan, and Lord Cardigan was cajoled into believing that somehow he would not be subject to Lord Lucan's orders. Full of his new importance, he enthusiastically made preparations: a noted Irish cutler was hired to sharpen the brigade's swords, and black leather patches were sewn to the seats of the cherry-colored trousers. The brigade sailed together with their horses, but Lord Cardigan traveled independently. He stopped in Paris to be entertained by Napoleon III and the Empress Eugenie at the Tuilleries, caught a steamer at Marseilles, and went to see the sights of Athens before arriving safely at Scutari.

The essence of the Crimean War for Lord Cardigan was not the conflict with the Russian Army but the conflict with his brother-in-law, Lord Lucan. Inevitably, if an army is to function, men must be responsible to their superiors; that his hated brother-in-law was actually his superior was a fact that Lord Cardigan brooded over, incessantly complained of, and never really accepted. There is no reason to think that either would have been a particularly good general on his own, but teamed together they were impossible.

The cavalry saw little action in the early stages of the war. Many horses had not survived the treacherous voyage out, and nearly a hundred more had perished of heat, overwork, and lack of forage on a reconnaissance Lord Cardigan had made to the Danube soon after his arrival at Varna. Lord Raglan was most anxious to keep his cavalry up to strength for future need, and the battles of Calamita Bay and Alma were fought entirely by the infantry. Under such restraint, Lord Cardigan began to lose interest in his command. When his elegant yacht, the *Dryad*, sailed into the harbor at Balaclava with his French cook and his great friend Mr. Hubert de Burgh aboard, Cardigan was only too glad to request permission of Lord Raglan to dine and sleep there every night. The army, of course, was enraged: was Lord Cardigan really to command his brigade and yet be allowed to escape the hardships of cold, bad food, vermin, and mud? They promptly christened him the "Noble Yachtsman."

The Earl of Cardigan owes his place in history to the Battle of Balaclava, which began before dawn on October 25, 1854. He and Lord Lucan each blamed the other for the fact that the Light Brigade did not pursue the Russian cavalry after the latter was routed by the heroic actions of the Heavy Brigade early in the day. Lord Lucan's orders—"to attack anything and everything that shall come within reach of you," but otherwise to remain and defend his position—may have been imprecise, but an experienced cavalry commander with a feel for his job would have realized that he must charge. Soon afterward Lord Raglan, on the heights above the field of battle, issued an ambiguously worded order, which was misinterpreted by Lord Lucan to read that the Light Brigade should charge the length of the North Valley, flanked as it was on either side by Russian batteries and riflemen, and that the brigade should assault the main Russian battery at the far end.

Had Lords Cardigan and Lucan been on better terms, they might have discussed this apparently suicidal order and reasoned out what Lord Raglan had actually intended. But they were not, and so the Light Brigade was doomed. Lord Cardigan placed himself alone some two lengths ahead of his staff and five lengths before his front line. He looked splendid in his cherry-color and royal blue, still handsome and trim, riding his favorite charger, Ronald. He raised his sword, the trumpet sounded, and in a strangely quiet voice he gave the order: "The Brigade will advance. Walk, march, trot. . . ."

Lord Cardigan's most redeeming quality was probably his dauntless courage. He rode straight down the valley toward the white bank of smoke at the other end, and as he never looked back, he did not know that almost the entire Light Brigade fell behind him. He picked out an opening between two guns in the center of the Russian line and rode steadily toward it. Miraculously, he reached it unhurt and galloped into the battery, having performed an extraordinary feat to perfection. Then he charged on until he was clear of the smoke and found himself facing, much to his — and, even more, their — surprise, the great mass of the Russian cavalry. Once more Lord Cardigan was incredibly lucky. The officer nearest him happened to be Prince Radzivill, who immediately recognized him from the many London dinners they had attended together. Radzivill at once ordered his men to capture the earl alive. Finding that he was not shot at, Lord Cardigan wheeled about, evading his pursuers, and dashed back out through the now-silenced guns just about where he had, only a few moments before, dashed in. He could not see his brigade anywhere, and only faintly aware that it was perhaps unusual for a general to be unaccompanied, he slowly and with the greatest dignity walked his horse back up the valley.

When the next month Lord Cardigan gave up the war and returned to England on the *Dryad,* he was acclaimed as the hero of the already legendary charge of the Light Brigade. The same fickle mob that had jeered him before cheered him now; the queen invited him to Windsor "from Tuesday to Thursday," and the woolen jacket that he had worn during the campaign was copied en masse, christened a "cardigan," and sold everywhere. He gave speeches at banquets in his honor, arriving whenever possible on horseback in full uniform, and speaking of the battle with ever increasing emotion. He was, briefly, the hero of the day. But the men he had left behind to endure the terrible hardships of that Crimean winter eventually returned, and in time the full story of his indifference, neglect, and lack of responsibility was revealed, erasing forever that fleeting moment of glory.

Retiring to his estate, Lord Cardigan took as his third wife the beautiful (if not quite respectable) Adeline de Horsey, the daughter of his old friend Mr. Spencer Horsey de Horsey. They lived very splendidly at Deene Park, where in the winter sixteen men were employed to keep the fires going and another twenty to store ice for the following summer. Lady Cardigan scandalized the neighborhood by appearing in Spanish costume and dancing the cachucha after dinner, but the earl was apparently very fond of her, and they lived happily together until he died at the age of seventy-one of injuries he received when he fell from his horse.

Châteaubriand (shà-tō-brē-än') *n.* Also **châteaubriand.** A double-thick tender center cut of beef tenderloin.

Fʀançois-René de Châteaubriand grew up in Combourg, a vast fortress in Brittany intended for an entire company of armed men. It was a gloomy place of few windows, high turrets, corkscrew staircases, and secret passages. The Comte de Châteaubriand relegated his younger son to the top of a tower; to reach it the boy had to mount a spiral staircase and circle the battlements. Below lay the hovels of a typical village of France before the Revolution. Besides his surroundings, the other great influence of his early life was women — not so much the ones he knew (chiefly his four sisters), but the ones he sought out in poems, in novels, even in the Scriptures. "There chanced to fall into my hands an unbowdlerized Horace . . . No one would believe the upheaval. . . ."

Châteaubriand was twenty in 1789, when, not long after his father's death, he went with two of his sisters to Paris. Peasants held up their carriage demanding passports; they found Paris thronged with nervous, expectant crowds. François-René watched the Bastille being stormed, and although sympathetic to the ideas of the Revolution, he abhorred its methods. He resolved to leave France. Carrying a letter of introduction to President Washington, this young Royalist with revolutionary leanings and passionate feelings toward the female sex (although he had yet to touch a woman), sailed for America.

The voyage took three months, but Châteaubriand was never bored. A fellow voyager described how during a gale, Châteaubriand, in imitation of Ulysses, had himself bound to the mainmast and was heard at one point to call into the wind, "O storm, thou art not yet as fair as Homer made thee!" Although he was not a religious man, on Good Friday he preached a fiery sermon to the crew with a large crucifix embraced in his arms. On fine nights he would sleep on deck wrapped in his coat and then climb at dawn to the top of the mainmast and salute the applauding crew below. One day in mid-ocean he took it into his head to bathe and was undeterred by warnings of crosscurrents and sharks.

Initially America disappointed him, for he had expected everyone to act the role of patriot all the time. When he visited Washington at Mount Vernon, the President invited him to dinner and listened politely as Châteaubriand outlined his plan to cross America in a wagon drawn by four yoke of oxen, journey up the California coast in search of the Northwest Passage, and then return eastward across Canada. Perhaps fortunately for Châteaubriand, a fur dealer in Albany persuaded him to settle for a less ambitious scheme. The young Frenchman allowed his hair and beard to grow, outfitted himself Indian style, provided his Dutch guide with a sheepskin toga and a horn to call the dogs, and set out—his only sure destination Pittsburgh via Niagara.

The journey through the forest enthralled him. He fared quite well once he had accepted the fact that the Iroquois could not be equated with Rousseau's "noble savage" and might truly desire his scalp. He roamed along the Ohio and upper Mississippi rivers for some weeks, taking extensive and precise notes about the wilderness. In time his notes came to interest him more than the land of which he wrote, and he found that he was more eager to be admired as the man who had explored the American wilderness than to actually continue to explore that wilderness. Almost penniless, he found a captain willing to take him on credit back to France.

But to be poor and a nobleman in 1792 was a dire predicament, and his sisters proposed the timeless solution—a rich marriage. They had just the girl in mind—Céleste Buisson de la Vigne, age seventeen, not exactly pretty, but intelligent enough. Châteaubriand, who loved all womankind, felt himself ill-suited for marriage, but family scenes distressed him beyond measure and he soon agreed. Not until after the wedding did Châteaubriand discover that his bride's wealth was considerably less than had been anticipated and that none of it would become available until she came of age. Such a beginning did not augur well for future bliss.

On borrowed funds Châteaubriand and his older brother, the vicomte, carrying false passports and wearing disguises, left France to join the Royalists' stouthearted if badly equipped Princes' Army. Châteaubriand spent some weeks encamped near Trèves, reading Homer and polishing his American manuscript, before the émigrés' single encounter with the Republican army. During the battle Châteaubriand was hit in the thigh by a shell. Wounded, half delirious with smallpox, he somehow managed to reach Brussels, where his horrified brother provided him with medical treatment and enough money to get him to Jersey, where he remained recuperating in a farmhouse until he was strong enough to join the émigré colony in London.

The French who made their home in London during the Terror were amazingly optimistic. After working ten hours a day to support themselves and their children, they would don all their finery at night for parties. There they predicted the imminence of a counterrevolution, which would enable them all to return home. Few of them fared better than Châteaubriand, whose exile lasted seven years. On his arrival he was pale and thin and spitting blood, and the London doctor he consulted told him frankly that he might last out the year. Believing he was dying, he haunted the tombs of poets and heroes in Westminster Abbey and languished in Kensington Gardens. But when he continued to live, Châteaubriand found it necessary to add to his dwindling income. By day he made translations from Latin and English; by night he worked on a comparative study of the revolutions of Greece, Rome, and France, a vast project that he hoped would start him on the road to literary fame.

Meanwhile, the news from France worsened daily. The king's head had fallen; Robespierre reigned; and one evening at dinner Châteaubriand heard an Englishman read aloud from the paper the names of the guillotine's most recent victims, which included his brother, his brother's wife, and all her family. Later he heard that his elderly mother had been arrested and taken to Paris and that his wife and a sister had been arrested and confined elsewhere. In each case the reason given for the arrest was "kinship with an émigré." He labored harder than ever on his *Essai sur les Révolutions,* which he finally published from London in 1797. "The greatest misfortune of mankind is to have laws and a government," he wrote. "All government is an evil, all government is a yoke."

When his mother died the following year, Châteaubriand, whose religious philosophy in the *Essai* had been decidedly anti-Christian, experienced a reawakening of religious conviction. It was no doubt sincere but it also happened to be in vogue. After the dry atheism of the Encyclopedists and the cruel irreligiosity of the Revolution, France was ready for a revival of Christianity, and Châteaubriand was more than ready to be the chief revivalist. He began work on *Le Génie du Christianisme,* which rapidly grew from pamphlet to book length. The book was already half printed in London when in the spring of 1800 Châteaubriand stuffed galleys and rough draft into his bag along with a Swiss passport made out in an assumed name and crossed the channel for France.

Châteaubriand returned home penniless and virtually unknown. He borrowed money to live on while finishing *Le Génie du Christianisme* and sought out his good friend and literary mentor Louis de Fontanes (who happened also to be the lover of Napoleon's sister) to praise the book in his paper *Mercure de France,* well before its publication. He read selections from it to the little group of literary friends who revolved around Madame de Beaumont, a lovely consumptive who had survived the Terror although the rest of her family had perished. Their enthusiasm encouraged Châteaubriand to prepublish a section of the book entitled *Atala,* or *Les Amours de deux sauvages dans le desert;* it was an immediate success. Wax models of its characters appeared in the bookstalls on the Seine, and the book was praised all over Europe as the expression of the new France. Exalting, among other things, the monogamous Christian marriage, *Atala* was largely written in the house of Madame de Beaumont, who was by then Châteaubriand's mistress. The *Génie du Christianisme* was published in the spring of 1802 and was received as warmly as *Atala* had been. In advocating France's return to Christianity, Châteaubriand was articulating the wish of the majority of Frenchmen. His long discussions of Christian art and poetry were strong; the chapters on theology were weak, for Châteaubriand had an emotional rather than a metaphysical turn of mind. Moreover, his understanding of sin in the Biblical sense was nonexistent; he passed from one infidelity to another throughout his life. Now the man who had written "all government is an evil" suddenly acquired a taste for politics and lobbied to become secretary to the French ambassador at the

Vatican. At thirty-five he saw himself as having fulfilled a great religious mission and as moving on to matters of state. "I came to politics by way of religion," he was fond of saying.

Châteaubriand got the appointment and in his eagerness raced off to Rome before the Cardinal, his employer. He toured the holy city, had his audience with Pius VII, and was feeling very much at home when the ambassador arrived. Then, most indiscreetly, Châteaubriand went to pay his respects to the king of Sardinia, who was known to be conspiring against France. The Cardinal was incensed and banished his secretary to the palace attic to sign passports. Châteaubriand appealed to Bonaparte himself, but the latter only commented, "Châteaubriand has his own ideas of liberty and independence. He could never enter into my system, as I conceive it."

Madame de Châteaubriand joined her husband on his return to Paris. Her twelve years in Brittany had left her marked from an attack of smallpox, sharp-tongued, and bitter — hardly the type of woman with whom her husband was so prone to fall in love. However, she was amusing and rather out-of-the-ordinary and soon collected her own following. Unfortunately she still loved her erring husband, and realizing the unlikelihood that he would ever change, she came to accept her situation with a kind of mocking patience that had its own charm.

Châteaubriand never remained for long in Paris. When the curly-haired, coquettish Comtesse Charles de Noailles traveled to Spain, Châteaubriand planned an elaborate odyssey from Greece to Egypt and on to the Holy Land that seemed only by chance to end in Granada. And then there were regular visits to a certain Madame de Custine in her castle of Fervacques. Finally, he bought a country home just outside the gates of Paris. To this hermitage, known as the Valley of Wolves, Châteaubriand would retreat to write. In the octagonal tower in the garden, he finished *Les Martyrs* and wrote all of *Le Dernier des Abencerages,* the tragedy *Moise,* and *L'Itinéraire de Paris à Jerusalem* (of which the Empress Elisabeth of Russia wrote, "I am a great admirer of M. de Châteaubriand; there is something magical about his style. . . . When I read the Itineraire, I'm often tempted to tell him of my flame").

Napoleon, who refused to consider giving Châteaubriand any government job, continued to admire him as a writer and was determined that he should be admitted to the Academie Française in spite of the opposition of the majority of its members. When the first vacancy came, a strict order was sent to the Academicians from the Minister of Police, and Châteaubriand was duly elected. But he was not about to allow his gratitude to compromise his Royalist views. His acceptance speech, in spite of its words of personal praise for the emperor, was nevertheless an indictment of the Revolution. Napoleon was furious and penciled out great portions of it; Châteaubriand refused to write another, and the matter rested there.

After Napoleon's return from Moscow, when the fall of the Empire seemed imminent, Châteaubriand wrote *De Bounaparte et des Bourbons,* a pamphlet in which he castigated Napoleon, praised the kingly line of Bourbons, and enthusiastically welcomed the invading forces of Russia and Germany as liberators. If discovered, the manuscript would almost certainly have sent its writer to the scaffold, so Châteaubriand hid it under his pillow at night, while his wife wore it under her dress by day.

April, 1814, saw the return of the Bourbons to France and the publication of the pamphlet. Châteaubriand had hoped that its impact would be sufficiently momentous to open doors of state to him. But Louis XVIII, a Voltairian and a sceptic, was not immediately taken with the romantic Catholic writer. Not until after Napoleon had returned and the court and prominent Royalists had emigrated to Ghent did the king appoint Châteaubriand Minister of the Interior —a rather vague position since the interior was at the time controlled by Napoleon rather than the king. After Waterloo Louis made Châteaubriand a peer, but again passed him over for an active ministry. Again the writer put his opposition into words. *La Monarchie selon la Charte* condemned the king's practice of employing men who had served under Bonaparte instead of only loyal monarchists. Against all advice he published the pamphlet in September, 1816; the king dismissed him immediately in disgrace. Châteaubriand was forced to sell first his library and then the Valley of Wolves.

On one of the lengthy visits that the Châteaubriands took to making at their friends' chateaux, Châteaubriand renewed his acquaintance with Madame de Récamier, whom he had first met years before at Madame de Staël's. Since then half the heads of Europe had been in love with her, but she had remained true to her aging husband. Châteaubriand courted her for a year and a half before she gave way. She exerted an enormous—and immensely beneficial—influence over him. It was she who arranged a reconciliation between him and the king, which led to his appointment in 1820 as minister plenipotentiary to Prussia.

To his delight he was transferred from Berlin to the embassy in London. It was there, in the great house in Portland Place, that his chef, the renowned Montmirel, invented for ambassadorial dinners the gastronomic delight that he dubbed beefsteak Châteaubriand, which he very likely fed to George IV when the king dined there.

Later, as foreign minister, Châteaubriand himself wrote all the voluminous and brilliant private dispatches that went out to the heads of Europe. But his colleagues were jealous of this writer-turned-politician, and Châteaubriand, aware of his superior intelligence and natural abilities, was haughty toward the other ministers. Then, too, he had become enamored of a lovely young lady half his age, Madame Cordélia de Castellane; for her he neglected Madame de Récamier, who responded by leaving Paris just when he most needed her wise protection. Thus it was that Châteaubriand was dismissed as foreign minister.

From his self-proclaimed post as leader of the opposition, Châteaubriand watched Charles X succeed to the throne. The new king found Châteaubriand to be still much too powerful and made him ambassador to Rome to get him away from Paris. Leo XII was overtly cordial, and embassy life was dazzling in its succession of banquets and fêtes. There was time as well for the romantic conquest of the French writer Hortense Allart, despite the presence of Madame de Châteaubriand and his daily letters home to Madame de Récamier.

Châteaubriand returned to Paris shortly before the Revolution of 1830 toppled Charles X and the Bourbon dynasty. When the Chamber of Peers met to swear allegiance to Louis-Philippe and the new monarchy, Châteaubriand attended but refused to take the oath. He laid aside his peer's robes, sword, and plumed hat and retired to face old age with the fierce nobility that was his strongest asset. His last years were no less eventful than the rest of his life had been; he went in and out of exile and was arrested and imprisoned for supporting the abortive attempt of the Duchesse de Berry to recapture the throne for her son. Châteaubriand wrote his memoirs and made punctual daily visits to Madame de Récamier, who survived his wife and was with him when, shortly before his eightieth birthday, he died.

Nicolas Chauvin

chauvinism (shō′vən–ĭz′əm) *n.* Militant and boastful devotion to and glorification of one's country; fanatical patriotism.

Nicolas Chauvin was a common French soldier of the Republic and Empire. Little is known about him. He fought for Napoleon, was severely wounded and mutilated, and received as compensation a ceremonial saber, a red ribbon, and a pension of two hundred francs (forty dollars) per year. A modern soldier might not find these rewards very exciting; but Nicolas Chauvin was not only satisfied, he was extravagantly, almost deliriously, grateful. Indeed his enthusiasm for Napoleon occupied so much of his conversation that his comrades could not but ridicule him for it. Hence, "chauvinism."

chesterfield (chĕs'tər-fēld') *n.* A single-breasted or double-breasted overcoat, usually with concealed buttons and a velvet collar.

Unhappily, the chesterfield originated in the nineteenth century and thus was not the invention of the famous eighteenth-century wit Philip Dormer Stanhope, fourth Earl of Chesterfield. There were, moreover, several nineteenth-century holders of the title, and no one is apparently willing to say which earl—or which earl's tailor—created the elegant coat.

clerihew (klĕr′ə-hyōō) *n.* A humorous quatrain about a person who is generally named in the first line.

As schoolboys, Edmund Clerihew Bentley and Gilbert Keith Chesterton wiled away many a dull evening by writing little rhymed quatrains on the prominent personalities they encountered in their studies. Bentley's first inspiration went

> Sir Humphrey Davy
> Detested gravy.
> He lived in the odium
> Of having invented Sodium.

The pastime was neglected when Bentley went to Oxford, where he was president of the Union and a member of a brilliant circle that included Lord Birkenhead and Hilaire Belloc. But later, when he was working as a journalist on the *Daily News* and *Daily Telegraph*, he again dashed off a series of quatrains that included the following:

> Sir Christopher Wren
> Said "I'm going to dine with some men.
> If anybody calls
> Say I'm designing St. Paul's."

He published them as "clerihews." About this time he also published the celebrated detective novel

Trent's Last Case, considered a milestone in the genre because it substituted for the romantic figure of the infallible Sherlock Holmes the more realistic and human one of Philip Trent. A quarter of a century later he resuscitated his hero for two more mysteries —*Trent's Own Case* and *Trent Intervenes.*

Although many followed Bentley's lead in the field of detective stories, the clerihew has found few imitators. Perhaps we shall be left with only Bentley's collection after all, including

Alfred de Musset
Used to call his cat Pusset.
His accent was affected.
That was to be expected.

daguerreotype (də-gâr′ə-tīp′) *n.* 1. An early photographic process with the impression made on a light-sensitive silver-coated metallic plate and developed by mercury vapor. 2. A photograph made by this process.

The new invention is blasphemous. For man is the image of God, and you can't imprison God in a little black box."

The year was 1839, the black box was the camera, and the invention of which the *Leipziger Anzeiger* so heartily disapproved was the success of Louis-Jacques-Mandé Daguerre in capturing a photographic image upon a metal plate and making it stay there. It was a hard-won success to which he had devoted the major part of his life, and that anyone should consider it ungodly no doubt surprised him very much.

Daguerre was born at the outbreak of the French Revolution, the son of a poor clerk of a provincial court. As a young man he came to Paris to seek his fortune; he studied scene painting and experimented with stage lighting so successfully that a new "Daguerre setting" in the theater became an eagerly anticipated event. Fascinated with the interrelation of light and paint, Daguerre and a fellow artist, Bouton, invented the "diorama"—a panoramic view painted on both sides of a canvas and lighted from

Louis-Jacques-Mandé Daguerre

behind. The dioramas were displayed in a circular building not unlike an enclosed merry-go-round. As many as 350 persons at a time could stand and admire as the floor slowly revolved past such scenes as a Swiss village nestled among snow-capped Alps, or Edinburgh by moonlight during a fire. The whole thing was much in vogue for well over a decade, and it provided Daguerre with the steady income he needed to continue his experiments.

The artist Daguerre's preoccupation with light, which culminated in the translucent dioramas, led to the scientist Daguerre's equal preoccupation with light and how it could be used to "paint" a picture. The concept of the camera already existed, and Daguerre was aware that two different processes were involved in making a photograph. First, a flat surface such as a metal plate treated with a light-sensitive chemical had to be placed inside the camera. Then, after "taking" the picture, the plate had to be removed and treated with a second chemical that would make the imprint permanent.

After much trial and error, Daguerre at last achieved a rather hazy impression of his subject on a silver plate coated with vapor of iodine that had been patiently exposed over a period of hours. His unsympathetic wife, who complained that he spent all his time in a studio filled with "malodorous vapors," consulted one of his colleagues as to whether he mightn't be losing his mind and need to be committed to an insane asylum. At her urging, the colleague, himself a professor at the École Polytechnique, visited Daguerre in his workroom, became as intrigued as his host, and advised Madame Daguerre not to obstruct the progress of science by interfering with her husband's work.

An accident finally enabled Daguerre to improve the clarity of the impression on his photographic plate. Having left an exposed plate overnight in a cupboard containing a saucer of mercury, he returned in the morning to find a beautifully distinct image — distinct, that is, until the plate was taken out of the dark cupboard!

About this time, Daguerre discovered that another Frenchman was working on the problem of fixing a photographic image. Joseph Nicéphore Niepce used bitumen instead of iodine, then dipped the exposed plates into lavender oil, which dissolved the bitumen except on those parts touched by light and left a fairly permanent picture. Something, however, must not have been entirely satisfactory with this procedure either, for although they formed a partnership which lasted until Niepce's death four years later, Daguerre stuck to his iodine-coated plates. Finally, after the diorama had been destroyed by fire, taking with it Daguerre's income, he discovered that sodium hyposulphate would effectively wash away the chemical coating on that part of the plate untouched by the sun and bring into clear focus the picture the sun had painted.

The daguerreotype was hailed as one of the wonders of the world. On the occasion of its first public demonstration at the Palais Mazarin, a huge crowd packed the hall, several people were trampled and had to be hospitalized, and the overflow waited outside for the first news. When success was indicated, the crowd went wild. With the exception of the *Leipziger Anzeiger* and a few other publications, the press was enthusiastic, too. An American reporter for the New York *Star* who was present at the demonstration wrote: "I never saw anything more perfect than that picture, literally painted by the sun."

The daguerreotype came into vogue quickly despite its disadvantages. The silver photographic plate was relatively expensive; the subject was required to sit absolutely still for fifteen to twenty minutes, and the image was shown in reverse, so that subjects were advised to part their hair on the opposite side and wear their wedding ring on the opposite hand. Not everyone was a suitable subject; the English writer Harriet Martineau writes of being part of a group daguerreotype, the first ever taken in Cannes, in which there is a blur where the peripatetic Henry Brougham (see *brougham*) should have been. John W. Draper and Samuel F. B. Morse brought the daguerreotype to America, where it quickly became the rage.

Daguerre retired to his native town, where he set to work painting the apse of the little church. He had had to sell his process to the French government shortly before he perfected it, so he derived little profit from it. Some professional bitterness, however, yet remained. "The sun, as it paints the picture," observed Honoré Daumier, "demands too much patience from the sitter. And patience is the virtue of an ass."

dahlia (dăl'yə, däl' -, dāl' -) *n.* Any of several plants of the genus *Dahlia,* native to Mexico and Central America, having tuberous roots and showy, variously colored flowers; especially, any of the horticultural forms derived from *D. pinnata.*

Linnaeus named the dahlia after his student Anders Dahl, a Swede who seems to have had no other claim to fame.

davenport (dăv′ən-pôrt′) *n.* 1. A large sofa, often convertible into a bed. 2. *British.* A small desk.

Davenport, the sofa, is a purely American term of conflicting origin. Davenport, the desk, is apparently named after its nineteenth-century originator, whose identity is still uncertain.

Derby (där′bē *for sense 1;* dûr′bē *for senses 2, 3*)
n. 1. A horse race for three-year-olds, held an-
nually at Epsom Downs in Surrey, England.
2. Any of various other horse races, especially
the Kentucky Derby. 3. *Small* d. Any formal race
with a more or less open field of contestants;
a soapbox derby.

Races had been held on the Epsom downs since the
time of Cromwell, but the town did not really become a sporting center until the twelfth Earl of Derby
came of age and took over the lease of The Oaks, a
converted alehouse. General Burgoyne, its original
owner and Derby's uncle, who five years later was to
surrender Saratoga to the American insurgents,
turned The Oaks over to his nephew to use for house
parties during the racing season. Lord Derby's love
of racing took second place only to his love of cock-
fighting, and both far exceeded his feelings for his
wife, the former Lady Elizabeth Hamilton. Lady
Derby, in turn, cared little for her husband and
nothing for the races, and even before their separation seldom went to The Oaks. Besides the four
Derby children, all Lady Derby really cared for was
the Duke of Dorset. But in their fifteen-odd years of
attachment she could never marry him because Lord
Derby, out of spite, refused to divorce her.

The earl entertained in great style during the
racing season. But while the guest list grew longer

each year, the meets were always the same — races for mature horses run in heats of two to four miles. For the sake of variety, the Earl proposed a race for three-year-old fillies over a shorter distance. A trial meet was held the following year and won by Lord Derby's Bridget. The earl was delighted. On his suggestion, three-year-old colts were allowed to compete with the fillies. That, too, was enthusiastically cheered. But what to call the race? Perhaps the Bunbury Stakes, after Sir Charles Bunbury, the foremost racing man of the time and himself a guest at The Oaks? No — all present agreed that it must, instead, be named for their charming and hospitable host. Thus the derby came into being.

The races at Epsom became more fashionable than ever, and the house parties at The Oaks more lavish. The earl did not always have a winner, of course, but his Sir Peter Teazle took the prize in the eighth Derby, and Lady Teazle won eleven races in all at Epsom. She had been named to compliment Miss Farren, an actress who was much celebrated for her portrayal of that role in *School for Scandal* and who became the second Lady Derby after the eventual death of the first. This last marriage proved a happy one — the earl's new wife was fond of racing, content at The Oaks, and unhappy only at the idea of cock-fights in her drawing room.

derrick (dĕr′ĭk) *n.* A large crane for hoisting and moving heavy objects, consisting of a movable boom equipped with cables and pulleys and connected to the base of an upright stationary beam.

The derrick was so named because of its resemblance to the gallows, which were, in turn, sometimes called derrick after the famous hangman of the reigns of Elizabeth and James I. Some say it was Derick who executed the unfortunate Earl of Essex in 1601, in spite of the fact that Essex had saved his life years before when Derick was condemned to death for rape in Calais. True or not, it seems clear that Derick expedited the deaths of well over three thousand persons during his long years of service at Tyburn.

derringer (dĕr′ĭn-jər) *n.* Also **deringer.** A short-barreled pistol with a large bore.

After serving his apprenticeship with a gunsmith, young Henry Deringer started out in the gun trade by making great numbers of squirrel rifles, which he traded for lumber with the boatmen along the Delaware River. The rifles spread all over the country, quickly establishing his reputation, while he sold the lumber in Philadelphia at a handsome profit. With the proceeds he was soon able to set up a good-sized gunsmith shop and to employ a number of apprentices of his own.

The excellence of Deringer's craftsmanship was best illustrated in the little box-lock pistols that he brought out in the 1840's. They quickly became popular with everyone from Philadelphia politicians to Gold Rush prospectors, who carried them in pairs in their vest pockets. The demand far exceeded the supply, and a California agent resorted to persuading gunsmiths who had apprenticed under Deringer to make imitation deringers. These fakes were signed on their locks "J. Deringer," after a tailor who received a commission on sales for the use of his name.

Foreign imitations signed "Derringer"—with two *r*'s—also appeared. In spite of such competition, demand for the genuine article increased, and Deringer was soon operating one of the country's largest armories. It has been estimated that he himself made approximately ten thousand deringers in the eighty-two years of his life. Stephen A. Douglas, the politician, always carried a pair, and another one was used by John Wilkes Booth at the Ford Theatre on Good Friday, 1865.

diesel engine (dē′zəl, -səl) *n*. An internal-combustion engine that uses the heat of highly compressed air to ignite a spray of fuel introduced after the start of the compression stroke. Also called "diesel motor," "diesel."

Rudolph Diesel was the son of a German couple who lived in Paris until the Franco-Prussian war of 1870 forced them to flee to England. Hardly had they arrived when Rudolph's uncle in Augsburg offered to look after the boy until the war was over. At twelve, Rudolph was therefore put on a train with his uncle's address tied on a card around his neck and sent via Harwich back to the Continent. Wartime delays extended the trip to eight lonely days.

Diesel remembered this experience well when, years later, he determined that all transportation would be improved if the not-very-efficient steam engine, with its clumsy furnace, boiler, and chimney, could be replaced by something considerably more compact. The internal combustion engine existed but in an imperfect state. Diesel was working in an ice-machine factory at the time, and among his patents for the making of clear ice and the making of ice directly in a bottle ready for sale were patents for improvements on the internal combustion engine, including devices to increase compression and elimi-

Rudolph Diesel

nate the ignition spark. Diesel constructed his first engine along these lines himself, but when he tried to start it, part of it promptly exploded and almost killed him. "The birth of an idea is the happy moment in which everything appears possible and reality has not yet entered into the problem," he noted dryly in his diary.

The experiment had proved, however, that a compression-ignition engine would work; the problem was to perfect it and to determine what fuel it would work best on. Everything from alcohol to peanut oil was tried, and experiments continued for years before diesel fuel, an inexpensive, semi-refined crude oil, was arrived at. As improvements were made, it became clear that the diesel engine had greater thermal efficiency and offered greater fuel economy than any other existing engine. When in 1900 Diesel met Count von Zeppelin (see *zeppelin*), the two men discussed the possibility of powering zeppelins with diesels. This eventually came to pass, but not until long after both inventors were dead. Ocean-going vessels starting using diesels right away, however; Nansen's ship, the *Fram,* was diesel powered when it made its Antarctica expedition in 1911.

His invention made Diesel rich and famous, and he traveled extensively. A few months before the outbreak of World War I, he was invited to England to attend an important congress. On the evening of September 29, 1913, he and two colleagues boarded the cross-channel steamer *Dresden,* dined together, and strolled up and down the deck before going to their separate cabins for the night. When the *Dresden* docked at Harwich the next morning, Diesel did not join his two friends on deck, nor did he answer their knock. When his stateroom was opened, they found his bed had not been slept in. The other passengers had not seen him; the crew found only his hat and overcoat by the after-rail. Ten days later the crew of another boat fished a corpse out of the water. The pockets contained a coin purse, a medicine container, and a spectacles case, all of which Diesel's son later identified as having belonged to his father. But in accordance with prevailing custom of "finds at sea," the corpse was returned to the waves and never again recovered.

doily (doi′lē) *n.* 1. A small ornamental mat made of lace, linen, or the like, and used to protect or adorn furniture. 2. A small table napkin.

Mr. Doily (also spelled *Doiley, Doyly,* and *Doyley*) was a linen-draper who during the reign of Queen Anne set himself up in a shop on the Strand in London and apparently became rich by selling various summer fabrics trimmed with embroidery or crochet work. Dryden refers to "Doyley's petticoats," and in the January 24, 1712, edition of *The Spectator,* in an essay entitled "The Ways to Raise a Man's Fortune, or The Art of Growing Rich," we find Doily classed with Scaramouch, the famous Italian comedian, and Rabelais as "hungry and ingenious men." "The famous Doily is still fresh in everyone's memory, who raised a fortune by finding out materials for such stuffs as might at once be cheap and genteel," wrote this early English journalist. "I have heard it affirmed, that had not he discovered this frugal method of gratifying our pride, we should hardly have been so well able to carry on the last war."

That Doily was also a collector of "curiosities" we have evidence from the *Philosophical Transactions* of the Royal Society of London, dated 1727. A certain

Sir Hans Sloane, a baronet and then president of the Royal Society as well as of the College of Physicians, writes there of "a Pair of extraordinarily large and strangely shaped Horns," which Doily had found "in a Cellar, or Warehouse, at Wapping, where they had suffered much by Worms and otherwise." These same horns, it seems, had been examined by a member of the Royal Society, a lecture had been delivered on them, and they were suspected to have been the horns of "the Sukotyro or Sucotario," an animal bearing some resemblance to the American buffalo. Evidently, Doily had displayed them for some time in his shop, where many people had gone to see them and where he had been offered (but had refused) "a considerable Sum of Money for them." The horns came into the possession of the president of the Royal Society only when the wealthy draper became ill. He was then attended by the eminent baronet "very much, as he thought, to his Advantage," and, concludes Sir Hans, "he made me a Present of them."

dunce (dŭns) *n.* A stupid person; numbskull.

King Edward I had only recently returned from the Crusades when Friar Elias Duns took his young nephew John under his tutelage at the Scottish Franciscan friary at Dumfries. John proved uncommonly bright, entered the order at fifteen, was later sent to Oxford, and from there to Paris to obtain his master's degree in theology. Inside university walls, Latin was the universal language, and scholars from anywhere in Europe could converse together with perfect ease. Known as Duns Scotus ("Duns the Scot" in Latin) by his colleagues, John studied under the renowned Gonsalvo of Balboa and lectured at Paris, Oxford, and Cologne. However, he was denied his degree until three years before his death owing to his stand on the age-old issue of whether the state did or did not have the right to tax the church.

King Philip the Fair said it did; Pope Boniface VIII disagreed. In the struggle that ensued, the nobility, the higher clergy, the University of Paris, the chapter of Notre Dame, and the mendicant friars all went over to the side of the king. The Franciscans, how-

Duns Scotus

ever, held out, and when on June 25, 1303, royal commissioners visited the chapter and examined each friar separately, the majority, including Duns Scotus, still sided with the pope. They were immediately banished from France. The pope responded by denying the University of Paris the right to grant the degree of master of theology. The dispute was resolved the following year when the king rescinded his decree of exile, Benedict XI succeeded to the papacy, and the University of Paris was permitted to award the Scottish friar his degree.

During his years at Paris and Oxford, Duns Scotus took issue with the doctrines of Thomas Aquinas. He incorporated the writings of Aristotle into Christian theology and followed the lines of traditional Augustinianism, but with innumerable nuances and clarifications of his own. He became known as the Subtle Doctor, and although "subtle" in Middle English meant simply "clever" or "fine," it was particularly appropriate considering the fineness of the distinctions between his and other metaphysical doctrines. He stressed a kind of "univocity of being," which translates to mean that there is a point of ultimate abstraction for everything that exists. Also peculiar to his thought is the concept of "thisness," by which Scotus meant that there exists a distinct principle of individuality, which foreordains that, for example, every snowflake shall be different from every other snowflake, although they all have a common nature as snowflakes. He took interesting stands in theology as well. He maintained, for example, that God could change or suspend the last seven of the Ten Commandments, presumably because the history of man suggested new prohibitions not known in Moses' time. (The first three, however, must remain, for it would be irrational for God to permit negative feelings or acts against Himself, and God represents supreme rationality.)

Duns Scotus is also known in Catholic theology as the "Marian Doctor," for he was the first to defend the idea of Mary's immaculate conception in Paris theological circles (in all probability it was the uproar created by this issue that caused him to leave the French capital for Cologne). The great doctors of the Middle Ages asserted that Mary, like all other descendants of Adam, had to be redeemed by Christ, who was conceived and propagated in the ordinary way. But Scotus disagreed. He argued that Mary was preserved from all sin, actual and original, by reason of the redemption of her son, Jesus Christ. A heated debate on this point continued over the next five centuries before Scotus' view was accepted and definitively declared a doctrine of the Catholic religion.

The "Dunsmen" or "Dunses" represented an important school of Christian theology until they were somewhat discredited by the humanist theologians of the Renaissance. According to the followers of Thomas Aquinas and other critics, a "Duns" or "Dunce" was a philosophical adherent of Duns Scotus, and thereby a hair-splitter who objected for the sake of objecting. Thus, by extension, a dunce came to mean one who, although fanatic about details, has no capacity for real learning.

Fahrenheit (făr'ən-hīt') *adj.* Of or pertaining to a temperature scale that registers the freezing point of water as 32°F and the boiling point as 212°F under standard atmospheric pressure. Fahrenheit temperatures are related to Centigrade temperatures by the equation $F = 1.8C + 32$.

At the beginning of the eighteenth century there were almost as many different systems of measuring temperature in Europe as there were men measuring. By the end of the century there were, to all intents and purposes, only three, the eldest of them being the one employed by the marvelously skilled thermometer-maker Daniel Gabriel Fahrenheit.

Fahrenheit was born in Danzig but moved to Amsterdam when he was orphaned at fifteen and eventually came to consider himself more Dutch than German. He preferred meteorology to the career as a merchant for which he had been destined. By the time he was twenty he was making thermometers, at twenty-five he was sending them off to distant parts of the globe, and at thirty he was traveling about to the glassworks at Berlin and Dresden to supervise personally the manufacture of his tubes. He was elected to the Royal Society and died at the age of fifty, still a bachelor.

Fahrenheit first used alcohol in his thermometers, but soon switched to mercury. The division of his scale depended on three fixed points: he designated as zero the point at which the liquid stood when the tube was placed in a container of ice, water, and sea salt. Its level in the tube when it was put into ice and water alone came to 32 degrees and was labeled the "freezing point." The third point was that reached by the liquid when the thermometer was placed in the mouth of a healthy man. Fahrenheit designated this point as 96 degrees. In his few writings that have come down to us he noted two difficulties: the experiment used to determine the zero point worked better in winter than in summer, and if the thermometer was to be used for sick people, the scale had to be lengthened, as he put it, "to 128° or 132°. Whether these degrees are high enough for the hottest fevers I have not examined; I do not think, however, that the degrees named will ever be exceeded in any fever."

forsythia (fôr-sĭth′e-ə) *n.* Any of several shrubs of the genus *Forsythia,* native to Asia, and widely cultivated for their early-blooming yellow flowers.

W illiam Forsythe was a gardener who deserted the intemperate climate of his native Aberdeenshire for the warmer, if less pure, air of London. After thirteen years employment in the Apothecaries' Garden at Chelsea, he was promoted during the reign of George III to superintendent of the royal gardens of St. James and Kensington. He invented a plaster that when applied to a previously diseased tree would stimulate new growth. For this contribution to the British Empire, he received the thanks of both Houses of Parliament and the honor of having the forsythia, which he may or may not have brought personally from China, named for him.

fuchsia (fyōō′shə) *n.* 1. Any of various chiefly tropical shrubs of the genus *Fuchsia,* widely cultivated for their showy, drooping, purplish, reddish, or white flowers. 2. Strong, vivid purplish red.

There is no one who does not know that there is nothing in this life pleasanter and more delightful than to wander over woods, mountains, plains, garlanded and adorned with flowerets and plants of various sorts, and most elegant to boot, and to gaze intently upon them," wrote Leonhard Fuchs in the preface to his famous Latin herbal. Fuchs was born only a decade after Columbus discovered America, and he studied medicine at Erfurt and later at Ingolstadt, where he fell under the influence of Martin Luther and converted to Protestantism. After the University of Tübingen adopted the reformed faith, Fuchs was appointed professor of medicine there. It was principally in the environs of Tübingen that he collected the botanical specimens that he described in the herbal and illustrated with more than five hundred woodcuts of extraordinary beauty. His best seller of the day, however, was not his herbal, but a little booklet explaining what to do against the plague. This appeared in London about 1530 under the title "A worthy practise of the moste learned phisition

Maister Leonerd Fuchsius, Doctor in Phisicke, most necessary in this needfull tyme of our visitation, for the comforte of all good and faythfull people, both olde and yonge, bothe for the sicke and for them that would avoyde the daunger of contagion." The seventeenth-century French botanist Charles Plumier named the shrub after Fuchs.

Luigi Galvani

galvanize (găl′və-nīz′) *tr.v.* 1. To stimulate or shock with an electric current. 2. To arouse to awareness or action; to spur; startle.

There are many versions of the story of how Luigi Galvani first came to experiment with frogs. The most charming has the learned Italian professor of anatomy at the University of Bologna preparing a concoction of frogs' legs for his lovely and beloved wife, who was ill. While dismembering the frogs in his laboratory before taking them to the kitchen, he placed the lower half of a frog near a crude machine that he used to produce charges of static electricity. The knife with which Galvani was working touched first the brass conductor of the machine and then the frog's sciatic nerve, which traverses the lower part of the spine and continues into the legs. Immediately the muscles twitched and the legs kicked, as if experiencing a severe cramp. The professor stopped, amazed.

Galvani's wife, Lucia, who was the daughter of the much renowned Dr. Galeazzi, may or may not have gotten her frogs' legs that evening, but she did recover, and she became as interested in the twitching frogs' legs as her husband. She had shared his previous investigations into the hearing processes of birds, the anatomy of the ear, and the electrical properties of the marine torpedo. But this discovery with frogs promised to be of much wider significance.

In the course of his experiments, Galvani substituted numerous other instruments for the knife and various other animals—both warm-blooded and cold-blooded—for the frog. He hung frogs' legs by their nerves from an iron railing on the balcony of the Galvani home during a thunderstorm, connected the lower tip of each leg to a grounded wire, and observed that when lightning flashed, the legs convulsed. The professor continued his experiments for years. Finally he was faced with two possible explanations—either the animals had an electrical capacity that did not die with their death, or the spasmodic movement of the frogs' legs was caused by the contact of the metal of the knife and the metal of the electrical machine before the nerves were touched. Galvani finally opted for the first theory, but he was so cautious that he could not bring himself to publish his findings until ten years after he had started the experiments.

The explanation of what he termed "animal electricity" touched off a chain of events the consequences of which Galvani could never have predicted. He was so familiar with the phenomenon that he failed to realize what a sensation would be produced by the announcement that dead tissue could be made to quiver with life. Perhaps, people said, this "animal electricity" of the professor's was actually the vital force of life itself.

But not far away at the University of Pavia, the physics professor Alessandro Volta (see *volt*) had different ideas. He had read Galvani's publication carefully and had decided immediately that Galvani had chosen the wrong explanation. In a paper that he delivered in the great hall of the University of Pavia, Volta explained that the source of the electricity lay not in the animal tissue at all but in the contact of the two dissimilar metals—that is, in the contact of the knife and the brass conductor of the electrical machine. In other words, "animal electricity" was nonexistent, and the frog was no more than a vehicle to prove that an electric charge had been generated.

Once his theory had been apparently exploded, the shy and disappointed Galvani would have liked to retire from the limelight. But he had not reckoned on his fellow scientists at Bologna, the oldest European university in continuous operation, who felt their reputation to be at stake. Italy was still a disparate nation of city states, and the rivalry between the ancient cities of Pavia and Bologna was strong. The controversy spread to the universities of France, Germany, and England, where practically every scientist took sides. Galvani's supporters, eager to prove his theory correct, extended the experiments to the decapitated heads of slaughtered animals and the severed limbs of executed criminals.

Meanwhile Galvani, anxious only to avoid any further involvement in the argument, departed for the Mediterranean coast to study the anatomy of the torpedo. In his absence, Napoleon invaded Italy, conquered both Bologna and Pavia, and demanded an oath of loyalty from all university faculty. Galvani refused and was therefore dismissed. The authorities later sought to reinstate him at the university, but he rejected the offer and died later in the same year. Although his theory was wrong, Galvani is not forgotten, for we are today "galvanized" into action in much the same way as were the legs of Galvani's frogs.

gardenia (gär-dēn′yə) *n.* Any of various shrubs and trees of the genus *Gardenia;* especially, *G. jasminoides,* native to China, having glossy, evergreen leaves and large, fragrant, usually white flowers.

Alexander Garden might be called a lucky man. The congo eel, which he discovered, was named *Amphiuma means;* the large collections of fishes that he sent to Linnaeus were also otherwise classified; yet his name is immortalized in that lovely variety of jasmine with which, as far as we know, he had nothing to do.

Garden was a Scottish-American by birth, a physician by profession, and a botanist by inclination. Charleston, South Carolina, where he lived, provided him with a successful practice and a society of refined ladies with whom to associate, but Garden deplored living "so far from the learned world" and carried on a diligent correspondence with other eminent botanists of the eighteenth century, including Linnaeus who named the flower after him at the suggestion of a mutual friend. The Revolution provided the great misfortune of his life, for while he remained loyal to the mother country throughout, his only son joined Lee's legion against the British. Dr. Garden never forgave his son, nor did he ever consent to receive his little granddaughter, Gardenia. After the war he returned to Britain, where he died of tuberculosis soon afterward.

gentian (jĕn'shən) *n.* 1. Any of numerous plants of the genus *Gentiana,* characteristically having showy blue flowers. 2. The dried rhizome and roots of a yellow-flowered European gentian, *G.lutea,* sometimes used as a tonic.

According to the Roman naturalist Pliny, the gentian is named after Gentius, King of Illyria, an ancient country on the eastern coast of the Adriatic. Gentius is said to have been the first to discover the medicinal properties of the plant, whose root was employed in the Middle Ages to dilate wounds and is even now used in medicine.

gerrymander (jĕr′ē-măn′dər) *v.* To divide a
state, county, or city into voting districts to give
unfair advantage to one party in elections. —*n.*
An act, process, or instance of gerrymandering.

The career of Elbridge Gerry was as meandering as
the map of the senatorial district for Essex County,
Massachusetts, after it was redrawn in an attempt to
assure the election of as many Jeffersonians as possible. He was a loyal American with the best interests
of his country always foremost in his mind, but he
often found it hard to believe that these best interests
and his own personal views could be anything but
identical. What is more he seldom could say for certain just what his personal views were.

Born to a wealthy Massachusetts mercantile family,
Gerry came under the influence of Sam Adams, who
goaded him into a revolutionary fervor and under-
mined the aristocratic conservatism on which both
Gerry's family background and his future merchant's
career rested. Gerry never resolved the contradiction
between the democratic beliefs he professed to hold
and the aristocratic life he continued to lead. As a result of this inner conflict, he was touchy and obstinate
to the extreme; one colleague charged that he "objected to everything he did not propose." His name is
to be found among the signers of the Declaration of

Elbridge Gerry

Independence but not of the Constitution, because it did not follow the lines that he, as one of the drafters, had proposed.

Under Sam Adams' tutelage, Gerry opposed British rule long before the Boston Tea Party. He openly advocated revolution and employed his not inconsiderable mercantile experience in gathering supplies for the Continental Army. He could be counted upon to know exactly where in the colonies any needed item could be found. At thirty-two he was elected to the Continental Congress, and although he opposed the selection of Washington as commander-in-chief, he faithfully supplied his troops throughout the war. The liberation of the colonies from the mother country was the one point on which his mind never wavered.

But difficulties soon arose in other areas. When he was ruled out-of-order on some minor point during a debate in the congressional session of 1780, Gerry gave up his seat in a huff and spent the next three years attempting to vindicate himself for the injury he felt he had suffered. After the Constitutional Convention of 1787, at which he had failed to have his way in the writing of the Constitution, he published his objections to the document. In the excitable rhetoric that was natural to him he predicted "a Government of *force* and *fraud*" from which the people would "bleed with taxes at every pore." As a result he was not a member of the Massachusetts ratifying convention and went about gloomily prophesying tyranny and civil war.

Surprisingly, he was elected to the first session of

the new Congress, but again his intransigence produced difficulties. He vehemently opposed the whole concept of a presidential cabinet, believing that the duty of advising the president belonged properly to the Senate. Jefferson's Antifederalists, who counted Gerry as an adherent, were much distressed at his enthusiastic support of Hamilton's financial system (he was one of the first stockholders in the Bank of the United States). Then in 1793 he suddenly retired and returned to Massachusetts to oversee the education of his seven children.

But two years later France seized several American ships, and in 1797 President John Adams, against the combined advice of his cabinet, sent Elbridge Gerry to join John Marshall and Charles Cotesworth Pinckney in Paris to obtain redress. Although Adams warned him that the Americans must maintain a united front, Gerry could not get it out of his head that he and he alone could prevent open war with France. The three Americans, shunned by Talleyrand, found themselves facing Messrs. X, Y, and Z (as they were later designated in official dispatches). When these latter gentlemen demanded money as a prerequisite for opening negotiations, Marshall and Pinckney decided to have nothing to do with them. Gerry, however, heard them out. Feeling that Gerry was obviously the one to deal with, Talleyrand extracted a promise from him to keep all forthcoming exchanges secret from his colleagues, and then formally announced that the French would talk only with Gerry. Marshall and Pinckney determined to leave at once, but Gerry remained, certain that Presi-

dent Adams would delegate him the power to negotiate a treaty. Instead, Gerry was ordered home.

He arrived in Boston to find himself labeled
"Jacobin," a term hardly less damning than "traitor."
For a time he and his family were ostracized by
society; he was kept under surveillance, and his mail
was regularly opened. He remained an active Jeffer-
sonian, however, and when he ran for governor of
Massachusetts thirteen years later, he won. Once
back in the political arena, Gerry displayed the same
contradictory attitudes that had marked his career
from the outset. After governing with moderation
for a year, he threw caution to the winds and denounced the Federalists as secessionists and pro-
British traitors. He turned them all out of office right
down to the local postmasters, and then began to
attack Federalist members of the clergy. The latter
group chose not to turn the other cheek, and the
Boston press soon raged with the controversy. In a
desperate attempt to retrieve his lost prestige Gerry
became party to the redrawing of the Massachusetts
voting districts to enable the Jeffersonians to retain
their majority. "Why, it's a salamander!" one Federalist exclaimed, studying the tortuous, reptilian shape
of the senatorial district for Essex county. "No," another rejoined, "it's a gerrymander!"

In spite of his maneuvering, Gerry lost his bid for
re-election. The Jeffersonians, however, rewarded his
party loyalty by making him Vice President under
Madison in 1813. From this position he presided over
the Senate with a peace and accord unusual to him
until he died during his second year in office.

grangerize (grān′jə-rīz′) *tr.v.* 1. To illustrate (a book) with drawings, prints, or engravings taken from other books. 2. To mutilate (a book) by clipping out its illustrative material for such use.

In the mid-eighteenth century James Granger, an unknown parson of the obscure vicarage of Shiplake, Oxfordshire, published his *Biographical History of England, from Egbert the Great to the Revolution, consisting of Characters dispersed in different Classes, and adapted to a Methodical Catalogue of Engraved British Heads.* The reader was to illustrate the many-volumed work himself by collecting engraved portraits and pasting them in the appropriate places. The idea caught on with leisured young ladies of good society, and the price of books containing such engravings (which those same young ladies delicately snipped out with their sewing scissors) more than quadrupled. Magnificently illustrated copies of the *Biographical History* still exist, one with as many as three thousand portrait engravings.

Granger himself was much beloved in his parish, although his liberal views caused Dr. Johnson to say of him: "The dog is a whig. I do not like much to see a whig in any dress, but I hate to see a whig in a parson's gown." Granger's most celebrated sermon was preached before the Archbishop of Canterbury in 1775. It was entitled "The Nature and Extent of Industry," and Granger later published it with this dedication: "To the inhabitants of the parish of Shiplake who neglect the service of the church, and spend the Sabbath in the worst kind of idleness, this plain sermon, which they never heard, and probably will never read, is inscribed by their sincere well-wisher and faithful minister, J. G." The following year, while administering the sacrament during divine service, Granger was seized with an apoplectic fit and died.

greengage (grēn'gāj') *n*. A variety of plum having yellowish-green skin and sweet flesh.

Early in the eighteenth century Sir William Gage introduced this plum from France to the gardens of Hengrave Hall in Suffolk. The eldest son of Sir Edward Gage's eleven children, he married the daughter of the Comptroller to the Household of Queen Henrietta and had eight children of his own. Since Hengrave was fertile country, it can be assumed that the greengage thrived.

guillotine (gĭl′ə-tēn′) *n.* A machine employing a heavy blade that falls freely between upright guides to behead a condemned prisoner. —*tr.v.* To behead with a guillotine.

There are unfortunate men: Columbus could not attach his name to his discovery and Guillotin could not detach his from his invention.

Victor Hugo

The plain fact is that Joseph Ignace Guillotin did not invent the guillotine at all. Conceived of during the Middle Ages, the instrument had already been used in such widely separated parts of the globe as China, Italy, Germany, and Scotland. In Florence it was called *la mannaja;* in Edinburgh, the Maiden. Guillotin's contribution was to advocate the machine's adoption at a particularly vulnerable moment in French history.

Guillotin was one of the relatively few physicians born in the provinces who was allowed to practice in Paris. He was of sufficient eminence to have been selected by Louis XVI as a member (along with Antoine Lavoisier and Benjamin Franklin) of the commission formed to investigate the cures of Dr. Mesmer (see *mesmerize*) and to rule on the validity of animal magnetism. After the king convoked the States-General and requested the views of learned Frenchmen as to its composition and scope (it had not been assembled for the past one hundred and seventy-five years), Guillotin produced a pamphlet on the subject,

Joseph Ignace Guillotin

which became one of the first political harbingers of the Revolution. In it Guillotin demanded both the correction of abuses and the representation of the Third Estate (bourgeoisie) by at least as many deputies as were accorded the other two Estates (nobility and clergy). The Parliament of Paris confiscated the pamphlet, thus increasing its effect and Guillotin's popularity, and in 1789 the doctor was elected a representative of the Third Estate.

When the States-General evolved into the National Assembly, Guillotin drew up six Articles directed toward reforming the penal code. The punishment of a crime should not, he contended, bring disgrace upon the family of the criminal, nor should the heirs of a condemned man be deprived of his property. But most important, the French nobleman should no longer be executed by the sword and the French peasant by the rope—where was the *égalité* in that? Each should die from decapitation. The doctor accompanied his propositions with a detailed description of a beheading device that was quick and painless. "The mechanism falls like thunder," Guillotin assured the Assembly. "The head flies off; blood spurts; the man is no more."

His discourse was greeted with exuberant applause, but the matter of the instrument itself was referred to the Academy of Medicine. It was not until two years later, on May 3, 1791, that the Assembly at last decreed: "Every person condemned to death shall be beheaded." At that time Dr. Antoine Louis, secretary for the Academy of Medicine, brought in a report that reiterated Guillotin's earlier recommendation. The report was accepted by the Assembly, and the instrument was named—either after the doctor or the king—"la Louisette." Legend has it that Dr. Louis, intent on perfecting the instrument, showed it to the king, who was mechanically oriented and who enjoyed puttering in his machine shop. The king, so the story goes, criticized the cutting blade, which, he said, would cut better if it had an oblique edge. Whoever ordered it, the fact is that the oblique blade was adopted and in that form fell upon the respective necks of Dr. Louis on May 20, 1792, and King Louis on January 26, 1793.

But to return to 1791. The instrument now had to be constructed, and the official carpenter of the courts, a man named Guédon, planned an elaborate one with chestnut posts and copper grooves, and sent in an estimate for 5600 livres. This was evidently too much for the treasury, for shortly thereafter a German mechanic—some say piano-maker—named Tobias Schmidt proposed a less luxurious but still efficient machine for 305 francs, "exclusive of the leather bag to hold the head" (24 francs extra). He got the contract, and the completed product was erected on the Place de Grève. The first execution took place at half-past three on the afternoon of April 22, 1792, three days ahead of schedule. The victim was a highwayman named Peletier. Charles-Henri Sanson, official executioner of Paris for almost a quarter-century, was well primed on his new role. According to the *Chronique de Paris,* an unusually large crowd had gathered, but the affair was so rapid that the spectators were disappointed and dispersed not at all satisfied with the improvements of modern science.

Ironically, the machine that was designed to make public death quick and painless, and therefore merciful, performed so well that death ceased to appear horrible at all. The instrument was really so decorous, so clean, that many Parisians were quite entertained by it. The idea was conceived one evening of beheading the stone saints that adorned the church fronts, and by the next morning the statues along the entranceway to the old basilica of Notre Dame had all lost their heads. Many songs were composed in honor of the machine, and it is believed that one of these was responsible for the replacement of the name "la Louisette" with "la Guillotine":

Guillotin, Physician, Politician
Imagined one fine morning
That hanging is inhuman
Immediately he devises
A mode of punishment
To take the hangman's place
So with his hand makes the machine
Which simply kills.
It should be named
The Guillotine.

On January 21, 1793, the guillotine was transferred from the Place de Grève to the Place de la Revolution for the execution of King Louis. Later it was moved to the Place du Trône, where in the course of six weeks it beheaded thirteen hundred victims. Few of Dr. Guillotin's colleagues in the National Assembly escaped. For protecting prospective victims whenever he could, Guillotin himself was arrested, but he was saved from death by Robespierre's timely execution on the morning of the 10th Thermidor.

After the Revolution, Dr. Guillotin returned to the practice of medicine and lived a comparatively uneventful life throughout the rise and decline of Napoleon. He died of a carbuncle on the shoulder shortly before the battle at Waterloo.

hansom (hăn′səm) *n.* A two-wheeled covered carriage with the driver's seat above and behind.

Joseph Aloysius Hansom was a bankrupt architect when he registered his design for the "safety cab" (patent No. 6733) in 1834. He had it built in Leicestershire and drove it to London himself. The safety features included a suspended axle, unusually large wheels (in the original hansom they reached to the roof of the vehicle), and a body close to the ground. Its appearance resembled a shiny black box on wheels. The driver sat behind—on the back of the roof, so to speak—leaving an unobstructed view in front for the passengers; this feature and the vehicle's extreme maneuverability soon made it the most popular cab in London.

Later, hansoms were used as private carriages as well. To see the number of smart hansoms that graced the West End of London in the 1880's one would suppose that Joseph Aloysius had died a rich man. In fact he never saw a tuppence of the £10,000 for which he had sold the rights to his carriages, and he continued to design houses, churches, and various public buildings until his death.

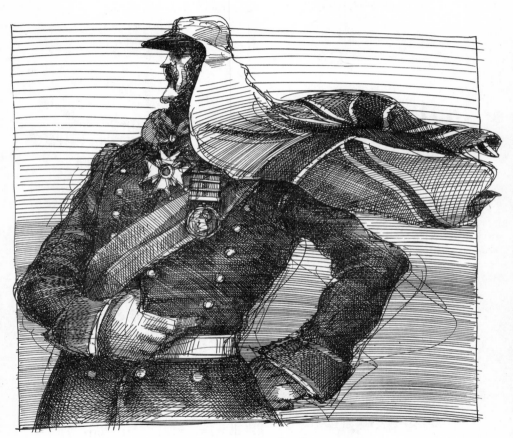

Henry Havelock

havelock (hăv′lŏk′) *n.* A cloth covering for a cap, having a flap to protect the back of the neck.

Even in the ranks of Queen Victoria's Imperial Army in India, Henry Havelock was somewhat of a misfit. He was, in a sense, English with a vengeance. He had not merely endured the severe discipline and humiliating faggings of the public school—he had gloried in them and had asked his father to remove him when a new headmaster instituted a more relaxed atmosphere. He had been unlucky enough to join the Army a month after Waterloo and spent the next seven years reading military history, absorbing the tactics of great victories, and shunning the lighthearted existence of the average subaltern. Then he decided that England was stuck with her peace and threw in his lot with India.

Young Lieutenant Havelock had hardly arrived at Serampore before he met and fell in love with the daughter of a Baptist missionary there, married her, and was duly baptized in the chapel. He appears to have taken to evangelism easily, for when he was appointed regimental adjutant, it was stipulated that he would *not* be allowed to preach. Instead he erected both Baptist and Church of England chapels near the barracks and expounded on the Scriptures at regular prayer meetings. "Havelock's Saints" his fellow subalterns called his disciples, but the commanding officer was grateful for even a few men not too drunk to answer a night bugle call. "Send for Havelock's Saints!" he was known to roar across the parade ground at such an occurrence. "For God's sake send for Havelock's Saints. You never see a Saint drunk when he ought to be on duty."

It has been estimated that in the nineteenth century, about three quarters of the British military in India were drunk three quarters of the time, which makes Havelock's crusade for temperance more understandable. He would hardly join a regiment (and he was a member of many during his career) before he would form a temperance society. Even more startling was his innovation of regimental coffeehouses as an alternative to the bars. After he had been in India for some years, his steamer was wrecked on the coast of Ceylon while he was traveling from Bombay to Calcutta. It was night, the surf was heavy, and rescue boats could not set out until dawn. Havelock's primary concern was that his fellow Europeans not drown their fears in the ship's bar. It is to Havelock's credit that after he spent a long night arguing the virtues of temperance the passengers disembarked sober the next morning.

In many ways his religion was more of the Old Testament than the New Testament variety. He firmly adhered to the maxim that might makes right, and he celebrated his first victory as commanding general by ordering the captured town to be plundered and then burned. Havelock's God was the God of Isaiah, except that He was British instead of Hebrew; He was directly responsible for all the victories, and Havelock thanked Him right along with the troops.

Havelock served thirty-four years in India with only a single furlough to England. He rose through the ranks the hard way, for he had no money with which to purchase promotions, as was the custom. He was sixty-two and a veteran of the Afghan and Sikh wars and the Persian campaign when he was at last made a general and given an independent command. "The saint," as he was popularly known, was viewed by his men as "sour as if he had swallowed a pint of vinegar," and was given to making high-flown, Napoleon-style speeches to the troops. But he proved to be a good general. He took command of his brigade in the early days of the Mutiny struggle, and his initial encounter, the battle of Futehpore, was the first defeat the mutineers had met in the open field since the rebellion began. He reached Cawnpore too late to do more than see the tragic results of the massacre, but after crossing the Ganges, he won eight successive victories before the decimation of his forces compelled him to retire to await reinforcements. The final drive to the Lucknow Residency was also successful, although again casualties were so heavy that Havelock's troops could only join their besieged countrymen and await further reinforcements.

The Mutiny campaign had been an extremely arduous one. Havelock's Ironsides, as the brigade came to be called, had fought against enormous odds, with sunstroke, cholera, and fever taking almost as many lives as the bullets of their Indian adversaries. They had gone into the campaign well armed with Enfield rifles but unequipped in almost every other way. Not only were food, medical supplies, and transport in short supply, but much of the infantry had arrived direct from the winter campaign in Persia in their heavy woolen uniforms and had no tropical clothing to change into. The best Havelock could do for them in the fierce heat of the Indian midsummer was to improvise white linen cap covers resembling those worn in the early Crusades, which were long in the back and protected their necks from the sun. These useful articles almost immediately acquired his name and an international reputation. In 1861, only four years after the Mutiny campaign, halfway around the world in Council Bluffs, Iowa, we find Mrs. Bloomer (see *bloomer*) of the Soldiers' Aid Society preparing for the Civil War by packing up 122 havelocks along with towels, cloth books of needles, and pillowcases, for Company B of the Iowa volunteers. Havelock lived to see the Lucknow Residency successfully evacuated and died in his tent a few days later in the perfect Victorian military manner. During a battle for a bridge over the Ganges, he spoke what might have been his own epitaph. When a soldier nearby succumbed to a round shot, his head smashed to jelly, Havelock observed: "His was a happy death, grenadiers. He died in the service of his country."

leotard (lē′ə-tärd′) *n.* 1. *Often plural.* A snugly fitting elastic garment originally worn by dancers or acrobats. 2. *Plural.* Tights.

Jules Léotard was a nineteenth-century trapeze artist who was featured in Paris at the *Cirque Napoleon* and the *Cirque Impératrice* and in London at the *Alhambra.* He seems to have been the first to perfect the aerial somersault, afterward predicting that all emulators would break their necks (an unfounded fear). Toward the end of his career he published his memoirs, for he was convinced that if he did not set down the truth about himself, some scurrilous author would be sure to print all kinds of lies. The little volume begins with an account of his infancy, during which time his crying could evidently be stopped only by hanging him upside-down from a trapeze bar. Also included are numerous examples of his fan mail and the text of a vaudeville play, *Les Amoureuses de Léotard,* which he professes to have discovered by accident in a copy of *Figaro* and which he labeled "truer than life." The *Memoirs* end with this advice to the gentlemen: "Do you want to be adored by the ladies? A trapeze is not required, but instead of draping yourself in unflattering clothes, invented by ladies, and which give us the air of ridiculous mannekins, put on a more natural garb, which does not hide your best features." What else but the leotard?

lobelia (lō-bē′lē-ə, -bēl′yə) *n.* Any of numerous plants of the genus *Lobelia,* having terminal clusters of variously colored flowers.

Matthias de l'Obel, or Lobel, was a Flemish botanist from Lille whose skill with herbs eventually landed him at the English court of James I as the king's physician. James, who prided himself on his learning, no doubt discoursed at length with Lobel in the garden paths of Windsor, and probably suggested naming the lobelia after him. Lobel died at Highgate in 1616.

loganberry (lō′gən-bĕr′ē) *n.* A trailing, prickly plant, *Rubus loganobaccus,* cultivated for its acid, edible fruit.

A native of Indiana, James H. Logan taught school in Independence, Missouri, in the 1850's and then continued his westward trek as the driver of an ox team for the Overland Telegraph Company. On reaching California, he settled down to study law; he was admitted to the bar in 1865 and later served ten years as district attorney of Santa Cruz and twelve as superior court judge. Logan was also a horticulturist. In 1880 he started an experimental fruit and vegetable garden and planted a row of wild California blackberries between a row of Texas Early blackberries and Red Antwerp raspberries. The second generation seedlings were duly planted and yielded an abundance of a new blackberry and a single plant more resembling the raspberry. The latter proved to have a unique flavor, and it was thus that the loganberry was born.

lynch (lĭnch) *tr.v.* To execute without due process of law; especially, to hang.

Most dictionaries still attribute the origin of the word "lynch" to one Charles Lynch, a Quaker, a member of the Virginia House of Burgesses, and younger brother of the founder of Lynchburg, Virginia. Charles constructed the first house of public worship in frontier Virginia, and as one of the leading men in the county, often arbitrated disputes over land, cattle, and other possessions.

This Lynch, who in spite of his pacifist affiliations was a colonel by the end of the Revolution, prevented local Tories from seizing stores of ammunition to give to Cornwallis, illegally tried them for treason, and tossed them into jail. However, there is no record of his having exceeded the law to any greater extent. When the Revolution ended, the Tories emerged safe and sound from their confinement and threatened to prosecute Colonel Lynch for his actions. He evidently acquired his etymological status some time later when historians, knowing approximately where and when the word "lynch" first was used, selected him as being its most prominent and obvious source.

Fortunately for Colonel Charles Lynch's historical

reputation, his almost exact contemporary Colonel William Lynch has since been found. Colonel William turned up in an 1836 newspaper editorial about the law on lynching written by Edgar Allan Poe. "The law, so called, originated in 1780, in Pittsylvania, Va.," writes Poe. "Col. William Lynch, of that county, was its author." Poe goes on to relate that in Pittsylvania at the time a trained band of ruffians was robbing and destroying property and successfully eluding the law. A group of neighborhood men prepared to take action as described in a declaration written by William Lynch and annexed by Poe to his article:

> Whereas many of the inhabitants of the county . . . have sustained great and intolerable losses by a set of lawless men . . . and that these vile miscreants do still persist in their diabolical practices, and have hitherto escaped the civil power with impunity . . . we, the subscribers, being determined to put a stop to the iniquitous practices of those unlawful and abandoned wretches, do enter into the following association . . . upon hearing or having sufficient reason to believe, that any villainy or species of villainy having been committed within our neighborhood, we will forthwith embody ourselves, and repair immediately to the person or persons suspected . . . we will inflict such corporeal punishment on him or them, as to us shall seem adequate to the crime committed. . . . In witness whereof we have hereunto set our hands, this 22nd day of September 1780.

Colonel William Lynch appears not to have disbanded his extra-legal law-enforcers until 1787 or 1788, when he became a member of the Virginia House of Delegates. Some ten years later he moved to that wild, remote part of South Carolina that previously had belonged to the Cherokees. There he spent the last twenty-two years of a life that had included fathering twelve children — three sons and three daughters by each of two wives. We would know little more about him had not Andrew Ellicot, a well-known surveyor, chanced to visit him in 1811. In Mr. Ellicot's diary, we read that William Lynch

. . . was the author of the Lynch laws so well known and so frequently carried into effect some years ago in the southern states in violation of every principle of justice and juris-prudence . . . the detail I had from himself and is nearly as follows—

The Lynch-men associated for the purpose of punishing crimes in a summary way without the tedious and technical forms of our courts of justice. Upon complaint being made to any member of the association of a crime being com-mitted within the vicinity of their jurisdiction the person complained of was immediately pursued and taken if pos-sible. If apprehended he was carried before some members of the association and examined:—if his answers were not satisfactory he was whipped until they were so. Those ex-torted answers generally involved others in the supposed crime who in their turn were punished in like manner. These punishments were sometimes severe and not infre-quently inflicted upon the innocent. . . .

Mr. Lynch informed me that he had never in any case given a note for the punishment of death; some however he acknowledged had been actually hanged though not in the common way a horse in part became the executioner: the manner was this.—The person who it was supposed ought to suffer death was placed on a horse with his hands tied be-hind him and a rope about his neck which was fastened to the limb of a tree over his head. In this situation the person was left and when the horse in pursuit of food or any other cause moved from his position the unfortunate person was left suspended by the neck,—this was called aiding the civil authority.

William Lynch was, Mr. Ellicot concluded, "hos-pitable and generous to an extreme" and "a great stickler for equality and the rights of man as estab-lished by law!"

macadam (mə-kăd'əm) *n.* A pavement of layers of compacted small stones, now usually bound with tar or asphalt.
macadamize (mə-kăd'ə-mīz') *tr.v.* To construct or pave (a road) with macadam.

Lucifer: I should like to Macadamize the world
The road to Hell wants mending!
Thomas Bailey, *Festus*

At the beginning of the nineteenth century all roads in the British Isles wanted mending. They were rubble granite causeways at best; at worst, muddy tracks. The main roads were built so high in the middle that when two or more vehicles had to move to the sides to pass they were often in real danger of tipping over. And the roads were so full of holes that the average life of a coach horse was three years.

Into this morass moved John Loudon McAdam, who as a child in Scotland had painstakingly constructed a miniature road system in his father's back garden — tiny roads built of small stones, perfectly laid out, carefully drained, and bearing no resemblance to the actual roads of his time. As a young man, John McAdam had been sent to a merchant uncle in the American colonies, where he did well in trade and married even better. Miss Gloriana Margaretta Nicoll, his wife, was a great beauty with a considerable fortune and a family estate that covered much of Long Island. But the Nicolls, the McAdams, and all their friends sided with the wrong side in the Revolution, and in 1783 found themselves on a boat bound for England, their American property forfeited to the state and their wealth almost all gone. On his return to Britain, McAdam's childhood interest in roads revived, but he had to lobby for years before he was actually entrusted with approximately 150 miles of roads around Bristol to see what he could do with them.

McAdam knew exactly what to do. He layered the roads ten inches deep with small, sharp-angled stones, which so compacted under pressure from the traffic that even the heaviest rain could not wash them out. The slope was just enough to allow the water to run off into ditches on either side. It was as simple as that, and before long the Bristol turnpike roads were attracting visitors from all parts of the country. Londoners came to admire and returned to demand the same. First Charing Cross, then the Quadrant to Piccadilly, then Regent Street, Bond Street, Saville Row—finally all of London's muddy arteries were converted into smooth and solid thoroughfares.

The rest of McAdam's life was spent driving about the countryside, overseeing the improvement of Britain's highways. But not everyone immediately honored him. The poet Southey wrote of the macadamizing of London as "quackadamizing," and a typical caricature of the period shows McAdam, wearing his kilt, straddling the intersection of the Great North Road and the Great West Road, with a caption reading: "Mock-Adam-Izing—the Colossus of Roads." But gradually the public became more appreciative of his familiar figure on the highways—

always riding in a closed carriage drawn by two old, bony horses and followed by a very pretty pony, all saddled and bridled for immediate use, and in the rear a great Newfoundland dog, whose job it was to keep the pony from lagging. By the end of his life, his contribution was recognized for its full value. "Macadamizing . . . became the symbol of all progress," wrote G. M. Trevelyan, and the socially conscious poet Thomas Hood lauded McAdam as

Dispenser of coagulated good,
Distributor of granite and of food!

Although he deplored the fact that

Thou hast smoothed alas! the path to the Old Bailey,

he concluded with elation:

We shall soon greet
Thy trodden down yet all unconquered fame.

mackintosh (măk′ĭn-tŏsh) *n.* Also **macintosh.**
1.a. A raincoat of patented rubberized cloth. b.
This cloth. 2. Any raincoat. Also informally
called "mac."

Although James Syme, later a famous surgeon, actually invented waterproof cloth at the age of seventeen, he felt it would be unsuitable to his future
profession to patent it. He left that to the enterprising
Charles Macintosh, a clerk-turned-chemist and a fellow Scotsman. Macintosh already had a number of
discoveries and lesser inventions to his credit when
he capitalized on Syme's discovery of the solvent action of naptha on India rubber. By cementing two
thicknesses of cloth together with India rubber dissolved in this way, Macintosh succeeded in creating
a waterproof fabric suitable not only for the raincoat
that bears his name, but for life preservers, diving
suits, fishing boots, and hot-water bottles, among
other things. Captain William Edward Parry, the
explorer, ordered a supply of waterproof canvas
bags, air-beds, and pillows for his arctic expedition
and later wrote in his *Narrative of the Attempt to Reach
the North Pole:* "Just before halting at 6 a.m. on the
5th July, 1827, the ice at the margin of the flow broke
while the men were handling the provisions out of

the boats; and we narrowly escaped the loss of a bag of cocoa, which fell overboard, but fortunately . . . this bag, being made of Macintosh's waterproof canvas, did not suffer the slightest injury." The Duke of Wellington tested Macintosh's fabric by placing forty of his soldiers on a raft supported by two pontoons made of the cloth. As a Scotsman, however, Macintosh's greatest contribution was the development of hose pipes for distillers and brewers which unlike the old leather ones allowed not a drop of Scotch or beer to escape.

Pierre Magnol

magnolia (măg-nol′yə) *n.* Any of various ever-green or deciduous trees and shrubs of the genus *Magnolia,* of the Western Hemisphere and Asia, many of which are cultivated for their showy white, pink, purple, or yellow flowers.

M*agnolia* is a tree with very handsome leaves and flowers, recalling that *splendid* botanist," wrote Linnaeus of Pierre Magnol. An exact contemporary of Michel Begon (see *begonia*), Magnol was born and brought up in the Huguenot town of Montpellier. As a Protestant he could not take a degree at the university there, but he evidently obtained it else-where, as he "practiced physic" in Montpellier for most of his life. That part of France was famous for the variety of its *flora,* and Magnol himself categor-ized the local plant life in a book that attracted bota-nists from all over France to study with him at Mont-pellier. Before his death at the age of seventy-seven, he published a systematic classification of all *flora,* which was later much acclaimed by Linnaeus.

Jean Martinet

martinet (mär′tə-net′) *n.* A rigid military disciplinarian. 2. A person who demands absolute adherence to rules.

General Jean Martinet organized the infantry of the French army into companies and battallions much as we know them today, and he instituted a degree of discipline theretofore unknown. He also introduced the regular use of the bayonet in battle. Voltaire gives him credit for inventing the pontoon; in any event he designed the easily transportable copper ones by which Louis XIV crossed the Rhine in 1672 — a much acclaimed feat that Napoleon later debunked as a "fourth-rate operation."

masochism (măs'ə-kĭz'əm) *n.* 1. *Psychiatry.* An abnormal condition in which sexual excitement and satisfaction depend largely on being subjected to abuse or physical pain, whether by oneself or by another. 2. a. The deriving of pleasure from being offended, dominated, or mistreated in some way. b. The tendency to seek such mistreatment. 3. The turning of any sort of destructive tendencies inward or upon oneself. Compare *sadism.*

The earliest memories of Leopold von Sacher-Masoch were of the dark and bloody tales told by his wet-nurse Handscha—tales of Ivan the Terrible, of the Black Czarina of Halicz, of Casimir III, called the Great, and his tyrannical Jewish concubine Esther—tales full of cruelty and torment, in which, more often than not, the tormentor was the dominating, lascivious female, and the tormented, the sentimental victimized male.

During Leopold's childhood his father was chief of police of Lemberg, the capital of Galicia, and he added to his son's education in violence with the tales he brought home. Leopold was ten when the Polish landowners staged an armed revolt against the Austrian aristocracy. He was twelve in 1848, that year of revolutions, and he viewed them from the bloody streets of Prague, where his father was then posted. His imagination was stirred by the ruthless cruelties of the times, and he composed plays about the revolts and acted them out in his little puppet theater. His dreams were haunted by scenes of execution and martyrdom in which he usually found himself the prisoner of some merciless, demonic figure.

Outwardly, life was calmer after Leopold's father was transferred to Graz, in southern Austria. The von Sacher-Masochs moved in the best society, and Leopold was their pride. The boy was granted his doctorate in law at nineteen and became a lecturer in history at the university the following year. He marked his coming-of-age with the publication of *The Rebellion in Ghent under Charles V*, an excellent history grimly ignored by his academic colleagues because of its readability and because its author was known to be only twenty-one, stage-struck, and full of wild ideas about universal freedom.

By the time he was twenty-five, Leopold had given up both history and law for literature. He seemed to be a normal young Austrian of good family, considerable charm, and growing literary prestige. But his European sophistication hid a maelstrom of primitive emotions. His subconscious was peopled not by the educated, civilized Austrians he saw every day, but by the fierce, half-savage peasants of his Galician childhood. The mother of his vivid dreams was not the delicate, accomplished madonna-figure who presided over the elegant Graz residence, but the robust, mercilessly bullying, fear-inspiring female of the Carpathian mountains.

But it is one thing to dream and quite another to act out one's dreams in the daylight world. Leopold began to do just that. Aware that his sexual impulses were outside the norm, he set out to find the nearest possible realization of his ideal—that masterful czarina who would bully and humiliate him, who would, in fact, physically *hurt* him. For pain, Leopold had discovered, was the necessary prelude to pleasure.

Leopold's first mistress was the beautiful Anna von Kottowitz, a woman some ten years his senior, who abandoned her husband and children to live with him, but who gradually lost interest in the whips and birches. The relationship continued for several stormy years and ended only when the new lover whom Leopold had procured for her—for he could not be entirely satisfied until she had betrayed him—turned out to be a crook. Leopold had found it necessary to write prolifically to maintain Anna in the extravagant style she demanded. He found he could write in almost any genre (except poetry, which he seems never to have attempted). He published many tales from his theatrical experience (he had done some professional acting), then a second history, and finally his first novel.

He had loved Anna, but he took on Fanny Pistor, his next mistress, much as he might have hired an actress for a limited run. The contract, which both parties signed, read in part:

Herr Leopold von Sacher-Masoch gives his word of honor to Frau Pistor to become her slave and to comply unreservedly for six months, with every one of her desires and commands. For her part, Frau Fanny Pistor is not to extract from him the performance of any action contrary to honor . . . is also to allow him to devote six hours a day to his professional work, and agrees never to read his correspondence or his literary compositions. . . . Frau Pistor, on her side, promises to wear furs as often as possible, especially when she is in a cruel mood. . . .

On a trip to Italy, Frau Pistor traveled first class as a baroness, while Leopold traveled third class as her servant, and in Venice, according to formula, she managed to deceive him with another man. She proved to be exactly the despotic, brutal woman he had envisioned, and the affair was really quite a success.

Leopold's best-known book, *Venus in Furs,* was written at this time, and its detailed exposition of his sexual philosophy made him quite notorious. The police commissioner's son became the subject of much gossip and the object of reams of correspondence from anonymous young (and not so young) ladies. He first met his future wife under a lamppost on a small side-street in Graz, where, heavily veiled, she had come according to agreement to recover from him a packet of compromising letters that a friend of hers had written to him. She called herself Wanda after the heroine of his latest novel, wore a long fur coat, and pretended to be very elusive. Weeks later when they were finally alone together, she went at him with a whip. Leopold was fascinated and agreed to marry her, although only at first in a private, unwitnessed ceremony to which he came dressed in white tie and tails and she, of course, in furs.

The marriage, later formalized by a public wedding, lasted fifteen years, but it was not a happy one. Wanda, like Anna before her, had not really understood what she was getting herself into. She was the daughter of a gentleman's servant and had simply wanted the socially prominent name of von Sacher-Masoch and the presumably enviable life of an intellectual's wife. She had not realized that this particular intellectual would insist on being thrashed daily with a nail-studded whip or that he would be so persistent about her taking a lover. In spite of the fact she was pregnant a great deal of the time, her husband steadfastly continued to parade before her a succession of potential "betrayers," always optimistic that his latest find would be a success. Finally, years later, one of his candidates—a M. Armond, alias Jacques Ste. Cère, alias Jacob Rosenthal—carried her off.

Meanwhile, through it all, Leopold continued to write. Although little read now, he was a leading literary figure of his time, and the twenty-fifth anniversary of his first-published work was marked by a formal celebration in Graz and public ceremonies in Lemberg, Prague, and Leipzig. By then he was living with a down-to-earth young German woman named Hulda Meister. They later married, and she loyally continued to care for him after his delicately balanced mind began to fail. Finally she had him quietly committed to an asylum after he had more than once tried to strangle her. Officially, he had died and was mourned accordingly, but actually he lived for another ten years, during which time the German neurologist and psychiatrist Richard von Krafft-Ebing read about his career and named his particular kind of sexual aberration "masochism."

maudlin (môd′lĭn) *adj.* Effusively sentimental.

Modern Biblical scholars argue that Mary Magdalen was not a harlot after all. They assure us that she and the repentant prostitute, whom Luke describes as having been so grateful and affectionate when Jesus forgave her, were two entirely different people. They would have us believe that the lovely sinner with the flowing hair was really only a practical-minded woman from the fishing village of Magdala on the western shore of the Sea of Galilee, a woman who devoted her days to providing for the material needs of Jesus and his Apostles.

But then why does she cry? Why does she weep bitter tears in every painting from Giotto to Georges de La Tour? Well, they say, she cries because she was busy annointing Jesus for his burial and had to interrupt her task when the sun set and the Sabbath began. And that was why she was the first witness to the Resurrection—she had gone to the tomb not to mourn but to finish her job. When she found the tomb empty, she never thought that He might after all have fulfilled His prophecy of rising from the dead

—right away she thought someone had stolen the corpse, because that is just what a practical, down-to-earth person would have thought.

Well, let us have none of it. The Mary Magdalen who wept at the feet of Jesus, who wept at the cross, who wept at the empty tomb—the lovely Magdalen of unending tears—let us insist on her. She may not be authentic, but she certainly has appeal. The word "maudlin," the old vernacular form of her name, could have evolved from none other.

mausoleum (mô′sə-lē′əm) *n.* A large and stately tomb, or a building housing such a tomb or tombs.

Mausolus was the wily satrap of Caria, a region situated in what is now southwest Turkey. Although in the fourth century B.C. Caria was nominally a part of the Persian kingdom, Mausolus was virtually an independent ruler who set up court in Halicarnassus and attracted Greek artists and men of letters to his residence. Outwardly espousing Greek culture, he was in fact and in spirit Asiatic, a crafty warrior with a large fleet at his disposal who coveted the independent Greek islands on the Asiatic coast. The only obstacle to his ambition was the Athenian League, a sort of ancient NATO, which, Mausolus reasoned, could be effectively dissolved if its most powerful members — Chios, Rhodes, and Byzantium — could be detached from it. Revolt was already in the air. Only a little prodding and material aid from Mausolus were needed for Athens' allies to turn against her. The resulting war so exhausted the great Greek city that she was unable effectively to protect herself later against Philip of Macedon (see *philippic*).

Then Mausolus turned on his allies, easily master-

153

ing Cos and Rhodes, and later adding Chios. All three lost their democratic governments to oligarchies controlled by the Carian dynasty.

Mausolus did not live long enough to enjoy his dominion, however, and the rule passed to his wife, Artemisia, who was called upon to complete the marvelous tomb that he had begun to build for himself at Halicarnassus. The greatest sculptors of the day competed to decorate this immense supersepulcher, which was by far the most important structure of the fourth century B.C. and was one of the Seven Wonders of the Ancient World. Artemisia reigned for two years before she succumbed to her inconsolable grief and, one hopes, followed her beloved husband into the great mausoleum.

maverick (măv′ər-ĭk, măv′rĭk) *n.* 1. An unbranded or orphaned range calf or colt, tradi-
tionally considered the property of the first
person who brands it. 2. A horse or steer that
has escaped from a herd. 3.a. One who refuses
to abide by the dictates of his group; a dissenter.
b. One who resists adherence to or affiliation
with any single organized group or faction; an
independent.

While still a young man living in a small South
Carolina town, Samuel Augustus Maverick saw his
father being rudely interrupted while speaking
against secession at a public meeting. He challenged
the young heckler to a duel, wounded him, then carried him to his own home and cared for him until he
recovered. It was a typical thing for the impetuous
young lawyer to do, but the provocation for the duel
persuaded him that South Carolina in the 1830's was
no place for a convinced antisecessionist. He had
heard much talk of Texas; Texas was the frontier of
the South—it was danger and hardship, but it was
also opportunity. He determined to go there.

Sam Maverick was thirty-two years old when he
first rode into San Antonio a few weeks before the
outbreak of the Texas war for independence. Sensing
the coming conflict, he walked about making mental
notes of the layout of the town and where the river
could safely be crossed. After the Mexican forces had
occupied San Antonio, taken him prisoner and then
duly released him (on the condition that he return to

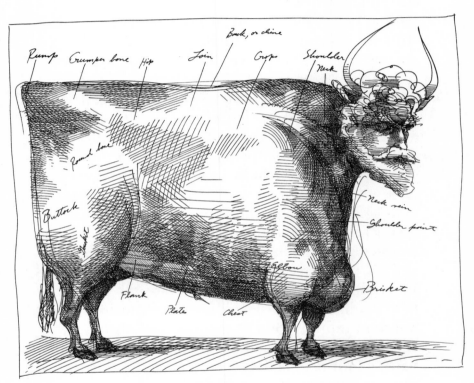

Samuel Augustus Maverick

the United States), Maverick rode straight to the main Texan force camped ten miles below the town. There he climbed upon a tree stump and harangued the troops, urging them to storm the town and offering to guide them himself. This he did, and five days later recorded in his journal: "White flag of surrender sent us."

This initial success led to his election as the San Antonio representative to the Independence Convention held at Washington-on-the-Brazos. There he signed the document by which Texas declared her independence from Mexico. Not until later did he learn that during his absence his fellow San Antonians had died, almost to a man, at the Alamo.

Rather than trust the mails, Maverick returned in person to South Carolina to reassure his family that he was still alive. There he met and married a remarkable young woman whose subsequent diary of their life together provides a vivid glimpse of Texas frontier existence. A year after their wedding, Sam and his wife Mary Ann set out with their baby, young Sam, and ten slaves (four of them children) for the new Republic. They skirmished with Indians several times on the way, and Mary Ann described another encounter soon after their arrival: "Our Negro men plowed and planted one labor above the Alamo and were attacked by Indians. Griffin and Wiley ran into the river and saved themselves. The Indians cut the traces and took off the work animals and we did not farm there again."

The Mavericks moved into their own house in San Antonio just before the birth of their second child,

Lewis, whom his mother believed to be "the first child of pure American stock born in San Antonio." Meanwhile, Samuel Maverick was buying thousands of acres of land and was away much of the time locating and surveying his purchases. He was apparently undeterred by the many rumors that the Mexicans were about to invade Texas, but when scouts advised that a force had actually crossed the Rio Grande and was moving toward San Antonio, he decided to move his family (there were now three children) up to the Colorado River near La Grange. In the autumn he returned on business to San Antonio, where on Sunday morning, September 11, 1842, he and fifty-two other Americans were captured by General Adrian Woll and a large force of Mexicans.

Maverick was held prisoner, mostly in Fort Perote, Mexico, for a total of seven months. He was chained, even while at hard labor, and was fed very poorly. General Waddy Thompson, United States Minister to Mexico and a distant cousin of Maverick's, eventually managed to secure his release from Santa Anna. He later described Maverick as "a man of fiery and impatient temper, who chafed, under his confinement, like a chained tiger." Mary Ann wrote: "March 30th, 1843, on Thursday morning our second daughter was born—child of a captive father and for him named Augusta. On the day of her birth, her father was finally released by Santa Anna in the City of Mexico."

The Mavericks' fifth child, George, was born in the year Texas was annexed to the United States. Sam had temporarily moved his family down to the Matagorda Peninsula on the Gulf of Mexico; it was there that he bought four hundred head of cattle at three dollars per head, the original herd from which were to come the "mavericks." Later that year the family returned to its old San Antonio home with its dirt floors, where Mary Ann recorded: "On Friday, December 24th, our sixth child, Willie H. was born. The joyous bells of Christmas eve were ringing when he was born."

When Colonel Jack Hays was ordered to open a shorter and better trade route through the wilderness to Chihuahua, Mexico, Maverick, always attracted by hardship, joined the party. Fifty men and fifteen Delaware Indians set out, lost their way, and existed on roots, berries, mule meat, and polecats so as not to starve. When no water could be found, they chewed the tops of their boots to keep their mouths moist. One man lost his reason; but the rest reached their destination and returned three months later, having surveyed a comparatively good road of some seven hundred miles.

The Mavericks built a new stone house in San Antonio, where their seventh child was born, and died. The following year Maverick was elected to the legislature. Their eighth child, Mary, proved to be sickly, but she lived. San Antonio was changing: the two older boys went to dancing school; there were church suppers; and when the United States Senator from Texas dined with the Mavericks, they went afterward to the theater at the Casino. Mary Ann joined a class in psychology!

In the year that the Mavericks' ninth child, Albert, was born, Sam took his sons Sam and Lewis, his slave Granville, and four Mexicans and set off for the Matagorda Peninsula to move his cattle to a tract of land called the Conquista Ranch, about fifty miles below San Antonio. The cattle were branded before the transfer, but they were wild, the range was open, and they soon strayed from their new home. Two years later, having no real interest in cattle, Maverick sold the herd to a Mr. A. Toutant Beauregard for six dollars a head. But the roundup was difficult, for while the cattle had lived on the Conquista Ranch, many calves had been born and none of them had been branded. The neighbors, who were not so casual about their livestock, had come to refer to all the stray, unbranded calves they encountered as "Maverick's," and the cowboys who rounded up the Conquista cattle for Mr. Beauregard cheerfully branded the unmarked yearlings they found as Maverick's, too. Sam Maverick never owned cattle again in his life, but Texas cowboys never again called unbranded cattle by any other name. Gradually the term was enlarged to include anyone who could not be trusted to remain one of his group.

The Mavericks' tenth and last child was born and died shortly before the outbreak of the Civil War. Samuel Maverick, who a generation before had left his home state over the secession question, found he could not at this late point in his life separate himself from his fellow Texans, and he cast his vote for secession. Moreover, he was one of a committee of three appointed by the Secession Convention to seize all forts, arms, and other belongings of the United States Government and transfer them to the Confederate Government. Sam, Lewis, and George all fought for the Confederacy; Lewis was wounded in the leg at the battle of Blair's Landing on the Red River and died a year after the war was over. Samuel Maverick died in 1870, leaving vast tracts of Texas land to his wife Mary Ann and his five surviving children.

mercerize (mûr′sə-rīz′) *tr.v.* To treat (cotton thread) with sodium hydroxide, so as to shrink the fiber and increase its color absorption and luster.

In 1800 John Mercer, aged nine, started work as a bobbin winder. When he was ten, a fellow worker in the printworks taught him to read and write, and somehow he learned music. Later he became a member of the local militia, and when he was assigned to the "awkward squad" for extra drilling, he managed to be transferred to the band. He taught himself the art of dyeing, and having become a handloom weaver, he invented several ingenious devices for weaving stripes, checks, and designs.

One day Mercer went from his village to the nearby town of Blackburn to obtain a marriage license. There he saw a copy of James Parkinson's *The Chemical Pocket-book* in a bookstall. A careful reading of the book enabled Mercer to enter a fabric printworks as a chemist. There his aptitude was soon rewarded by a partnership and considerable financial profit. After thirty years the firm was dissolved, and Mercer was free to continue his researches. It was then that he experimented with the reaction of caustic soda, sulphuric acid, and zinc chloride on cotton cloth and paper. The process he invented became known as mercerizing—strengthening of the individual cotton fibers by bathing them in a solution of any one of these reagents. Cloth so treated also proved to absorb dye much more readily. The importance of this discovery to England's fabric industry, and Mercer's anticipation of Pasteur's germ theory (see *pasteurize*), led to his election to the Royal Society. Mercer served as a local commissioner of Justice, but his compassion for each offender gave rise to this tongue twister: "Mr. Mercer is too merciful for a magistrate."

Franz Anton Mesmer

mesmerize (mĕz′mə-rīz′) *tr.v.* 1. To hypnotize.
2. To enthrall.

This magnetic stone
Should give the traveler pause.
Once it was used by Mesmer,
Who was born
In Germany's green fields,
And who won great fame
In France,   sings Despina in *Così fan tutte*.

It was, no doubt, Mozart's graceful way of thanking
Dr. Mesmer, his father's old friend and his own benefactor, for his early aid. For when the emperor had
commanded the performance of the fourteen-year-
old Mozart's first opera, the director of the Imperial
Opera House had refused to produce it, and Mesmer
had come to the rescue by offering the little theater
in his own garden by the Danube. There it was that
Bastien and Bastienne was first played, as were many
works by Haydn and Gluck, who like the young Mozart were intimates of Mesmer's house. And as one
walked under the great trees, near the dovecote, or
around the marble fountain, the sweet strains of the
glass harmonica could nearly always be heard. It was
an instrument that Mesmer himself loved to play;
Mozart composed a special quintet for it.

But to return to the magnetic stone. . . .

Franz Anton Mesmer of Vienna had studied philosophy, then law, then medicine, and held doctorates
in all three. Because later he was so often viewed as a
dilettante and a humbug, it is important to remember

165

that he was a truly learned man in the Renaissance tradition, and he had the Renaissance fascination with the influence of the planets on the human body. All his life he was possessed by the idea of a magic, magnetic, invisible fluid, in which all bodies were immersed and through which the planets exerted their influence. The exact nature of this fluid always eluded him, but he was so convinced of its existence that he could not give up his belief in it, even after he realized that he had actually discovered something else entirely — a new treatment for the human psyche.

The magnet was the important instrument in all Mesmer's early experiments. He wore one in a little leather sack around his neck and spent every free moment experimenting with it on everything he saw. He believed that inanimate objects were capable of transferring beneficent powers to human beings through the magic fluid that surrounded them; therefore he magnetized cups and plates, clothes, mirrors, beds and bedcovers, even his patients' bath water. He further believed that this magnetic fluid would travel along wires and so he constructed his famous "baquet" — a large wooden tub of magnetized water having a lid pierced with holes. Through the holes emerged jointed steel rods, which the patients applied to the ailing parts of their bodies. Nothing was ever done privately; a number of patients would afterward gather around the "baquet" and hold hands in order to increase the potency of the fluid. Mesmer magnetized the trees in his garden and the water in the basin of his fountain. Then he would seat his patients around the fountain and have them bathe their feet in the water while grasping cables that were connected to the magnetized trees. Meanwhile Mesmer would strike soothing notes on his magnetized musical glasses until he deemed that day's treatment complete.

Inevitably, some people were cured. The news spread, and the multitudes came. The magnet became the cure-all for such diverse ailments as gout and ear troubles, spasms and insomnia, paralysis and stomachache. Then, just as Mesmer's fame was spreading throughout Austria and beyond—just after he was made a member of the Academy of the Sciences of Electoral Bavaria for having discovered the miraculous possibilities of the common magnet—just then did Mesmer begin to realize that the magnet actually had nothing to do with his cures. He found by experiment that his patients improved whether or not he held the magnet in his hand. The cure was not in the magnet at all; it was in the stroking movement of his hand. That is, it was in him.

But what to do? Go before the Academy of the Sciences of Electoral Bavaria and tell them it was all a mistake? A laboratory scientist might have done so, but Mesmer was not a laboratory scientist. He was a Renaissance humanist and he believed he could somehow incorporate this new discovery within the old hypothesis. The theory of the magnet had proved misguided, he allowed, but the theory of magnetism was as valid as ever. It was just a slightly altered type of magnetism: it was animal magnetism! The "animal" was the living human being who could exert powers over his kind as strong and mysterious as the powers of the dead magnet over dead metal.

Poor Mesmer! His world was not ready for him. It was not yet 1776—much less 1789—and the established order of things had not yet been disrupted. The same authorities who had been willing to accept the idea that there might be curative properties within a lifeless magnet were not at all willing to admit that the mere presence of a living man could have the same effect. They were especially embittered to find that Mesmer continued to be so successful in his cures; in fact, patients flocked to him in about the same proportion that official opposition mounted against him. But the officials, not the patients, held the power; first Cardinal Migazzi, then Empress Maria Theresa and the court, and finally the famous Committee to Sustain Morality mobilized against him. Mesmer left Vienna for Switzerland and then for Paris. The case for psychology had lost the first round.

Mesmer wanted one thing only: to have his method validated by the official scientific world. In Paris that world was represented by the Academy of Sciences. He wanted the academicians simply to see for themselves what miracles could be worked in a nervous, distraught patient by the mere manipulation of the fingertips. It was not enough for Mesmer that the Prince de Condé, the Duc de Bourbon, the Baron de Montesquieu, the young Marquis de Lafayette, and Queen Marie Antoinette were won over to his cause, or even that the influential Dr. Charles Deslon, physician-in-ordinary to the Comte d'Artois, supported him. When the Academy declined to recognize him, he left Paris. His self-exile quickly became an affair of state; public indignation with the Academy ran high, and a joint stock company was formed to provide Mesmer with funds so that he could return to Paris and continue his research. Lafayette, on the eve of his departure, wrote General Washington that he was bringing not only cannon and other weapons with him, but also "le secret de Mesmer," which he had received permission to confide to Washington. Mesmer returned to Paris in triumph.

Unfortunately, the public acclaim of the fashionable world has rarely furthered the cause of science. There is no question that had he been given a choice, Mesmer would have preferred scientific to social recognition. But no choice was offered him; his practice in Paris was now the vogue, "la grande mode"; appointments had to be made days in advance for treatment in his main quarters on the Place Vendôme. The ceremonial of a religious ritual was established: windows were darkened to create a twilight effect inside, sound was deadened by thick carpets and wall hangings, and the famous "baquet" in the middle of the room was surrounded by all the silence and mystery of the altar at Notre Dame. Mesmer wore a lilac-colored robe and carried a little wand in his hand. For about an hour the participants would sit together around the tub as in a séance, while soft music played from an unseen source. Then Mesmer would approach each patient in turn, fix him with a piercing gaze, question him about his ailment, and stroke him with the wand. Eventually the tension would become unbearable, somebody would begin to tremble, somebody else would twitch convulsively, and before long most of those present would be caught up in the onset of the famous crisis, which Mesmer had come to believe was necessary for the cure. Some would go into convulsions, fall to the ground, laugh shrilly, or scream, or choke, or groan, or even dance; others would faint or sink into a kind of hypnotic sleep. It was no wonder that enthusiasm for Mesmer began to assume the proportions of a religious mania.

Mesmer's aristocratic following did not, however, include the king. Louis XVI was not fond of excitement and he was not at all taken by what he heard about the happenings at the Place Vendôme, or by the celebrated Dr. Mesmer himself, whom he referred to as "the apothecary." He was particularly tired of listening to the endless disputes as to the validity of "animal magnetism." So Louis appointed a commission of inquiry to settle the matter. This august body included, among others, a certain Dr. Guillotin (see *guillotine*) and an American visitor, Benjamin Franklin. At the conclusion of their investigation, the members of the commission declared that they could find no explanation for the phenomena they had witnessed, but they agreed without any doubt that animal magnetism was null and void, since "where nothing is to be seen, or to be felt, or to be smelt, there nothing can exist." Moreover, they concluded, Mesmer's methods constituted a danger to society.

One would suppose that after such discredit Mesmer would once again have left Paris. But apparently he did not. He had set up a treatment center for the poor in the rue Montmartre, which he evidently continued to operate until it was destroyed in the Revolution. When Robespierre came to power, Mesmer, poor and forgotten, fled Paris. Finding Vienna still closed to him, he took refuge in Switzerland, where he set up a more-or-less conventional medical practice in the little town of Frauenfeld. His patients were tradesmen and peasants who had never heard of Franz Anton Mesmer or animal magnetism.

There he continued to work, but in such obscurity that when, two decades later, the Berlin Academy of Science began to reinvestigate animal magnetism, its members were amazed to learn that Mesmer was still alive. Perhaps he would come to Berlin; an eloquent invitation was dispatched to Frauenfeld, but Mesmer declined. He was too old and weary to make such a trip. To an emissary from Berlin Mesmer demonstrated his method and delivered what written records he still possessed. Three years later he died, pressing his beloved glass harmonica to his heart.

Although Mesmer obviously practiced hypnotism, or "mesmerism," in Paris, he evidently never did so intentionally, for his object was always to produce a convulsive crisis rather than a hypnotic sleep. It was left to one of his pupils, Puységur, to actually identify —and name—the practice; Mesmer had quite failed to recognize the extraordinary phenomenon that bears his name.

napoleon (nə-pō′lē-ən) *n.* A rectangular piece of pastry, iced on top, with crisp, flaky layers filled with custard cream.

Contrary to popular belief, Napoleon did not carry a stock of napoleons in his inside breast pocket during his retreat from Moscow. It is even possible that he never tasted one, for the delicacy is actually Italian. The name is a corruption of "Napolitain," which refers to the Neopolitan custom of making sweets and ices in layers of alternating texture and color, and it has nothing whatsoever to do with the emperor.

nicotine (nĭk′ə-tēn′) *n.* A poisonous alkaloid, $C_5H_4NC_4H_7NCH_3$, derived from the tobacco plant, used in medicine and as an insecticide. From *nicotiana,* any of various flowering tobacco plants of the genus *Nicotiana,* native to the Americas.

In 1559 Francis II, the sixteen-year-old King of France, determined that his sister, Marguerite of Valois, aged six, should marry Don Sebastian, the King of Portugal, aged five. To conduct the delicate negotiations he appointed one of his ablest ministers, Jean Nicot, a notary's son of uncommon ability. Nicot was only twenty-nine, but he was a cultivated man of letters. He had begun a dictionary of the French language and had made an excellent impression on the austere Queen Catherine, mother of the young King of Portugal. Despite the abilities of the young ambassador, the negotiations failed, and the following year Francis died. However, the mission was not a complete failure. While visiting the Royal Pharmacy in Lisbon, Nicot had been given a strange plant recently brought from Florida. He cultivated it with great care, and before he left Portugal he sent back to the queen mother, Catherine de Médicis, the first harvest of his tobacco plant.

It was a well-calculated gift, for Nicot had observed in Lisbon the happy effects that the "American pow-

Jean Nicot

der" had on the general disposition of its adherents, and he also knew just how somber and bad-tempered Catherine could be. Just as he had hoped, Catherine became an enthusiastic user of what she termed the "ambassador's powder" and made it so fashionable that soon no one dared appear at court without fidgeting carelessly with his fancy box of tobacco.

Nicot also sent a small package of the powder to his friend, the Father Superior of Malta. With remarkable perspicacity he had foreseen how precious a diversion tobacco might prove to be for monks, who were endlessly occupied with songs, prayers, and responses. Nicot's friend was so zealous in spreading the use of tobacco in his order that the monks soon called it the Father Superior's powder. Nicot then returned to Paris with a whole cargo of tobacco, which proved to be a most solid foundation on which to build his fortune. It also brought him such notoriety that he became as much in fashion as the plant, which was soon referred to as nicotiana by everyone.

But fashions are fickle, and after the initial period of enthusiasm came the period of persecution. The first enemy was Scotland's James VI (soon to become James I of England), who fought Nicot's plant as well as papism throughout his life. Don Bartholomew of the Camara, Bishop of Granada, was offended by the discreet sneezing of his flock during his sermons. A profound theological dispute arose under Pope Urban VIII: Does a pinch of snuff savored through the nose break a fast? Pope Innocent X even went so far as to excommunicate tobacco-users.

Tobacco divided the Sorbonne and became yet

another bone of contention between the Jansenists (who were for it) and the Jesuits (who were decidedly against it). The Jesuits finally conceded that tobacco might not be forbidden fruit in itself, but only when used for the satisfaction of depraved desires; that is, only those *intentionally* defying God's command by sniffing or smoking would be excommunicated! Outside France things were even worse. Amurat IV condemned smokers to death; the Czar ordered that their noses be cut off; the Shah Sífi simply had them impaled. In Switzerland the Senate of Berne had "smoking" inserted with "stealing" and "killing" in the ten commandments.

But suddenly France discovered that a simple state tax of two francs per hundred pounds of tobacco brought in approximately one million francs each year. Tobacco returned to favor, at least with the government. Nicot was able to turn his attention back to his beloved dictionary, the oldest in the French language, which was finally printed in 1600, six years after his death.

ohm (ōm) *n.* A unit of electrical resistance equal to that of a conductor in which a current of one ampere is produced by a potential of one volt across its terminals.

When Georg Simon Ohm and his brother Martin asked their father if they might attend the university, he replied that they might do so with his blessing if they would become skilled locksmiths as well. Martin Ohm, Sr., a good German burgher, knew that however much he might have enjoyed his own extensive study of mathematics and philosophy, it was his occupation as a journeyman locksmith that fed and clothed his family, just as it had fed his father's and his father's father's family before him.

Martin, Jr. carried on the ancestral trade; but Georg Simon studied physics, obtained the degree of doctor of philosophy at twenty-two, and prepared to support himself by teaching—a much more precarious profession than that of locksmith. He lived an impoverished tutor's life, his repeated letters to the King of Bavaria for better employment having no effect, until the publication of his first book (copies of which he sent to all reigning monarchs of the German states) resulted in his being taken up by the King of Prussia. Friedrich Wilhelm invited him to teach at the Royal Konsistorium in Cologne, where research apparatus was readily available. It was there that Ohm arrived at his theory of electric circuits, which is now known as Ohm's law. When the International Electrical Congress met in 1893 — thirty-nine years after Georg Simon's death — to assign names to the various electrical units of measure, they created the "ohm" and its charming counterpart "ohmage."

pasteurize (păs′chə-rīz′) *tr.v.* To destroy most disease-producing microorganisms and limit fermentation in milk, beer, and other liquids by partial or complete sterilization.

When he was sixteen, Louis Pasteur thought he might become a painter. As a boy growing up in Arbois, he had painted his father, a tanner, and his mother—she wears a white bonnet, a blue-green checked shawl, and a determined expression on her face. He had also attempted pastels, drawing, and lithography, noting every detail of his subjects. But his other great interest—science—triumphed.

Pasteur entered the École Normale to study chemistry. He was a fellow there when the Revolution of 1848 broke out. Although sternly admonished by his father to stay home and keep away from political activities, Pasteur, to whom the cause of the Republic was sacred, enlisted in the National Guard and before long handed over his entire savings of 250 francs to its treasury.

After leaving the École Normale, Pasteur joined the faculty of sciences first at Dijon, and soon after at Strasbourg, where he quickly became attracted to Marie Laurent, the rector's daughter. He dispatched a letter to her parents frankly admitting his poor financial position, expressing his determination to devote his life to chemical research, and concluding, "My father will come to Strasbourg to make a proposal of marriage." Marie's father considered him rather impudent and did not answer his letter. In desperation Pasteur appealed to Madame Laurent, who eventually brought the rector around. Pasteur and Marie were married on May 29, 1849.

While at Strasbourg Pasteur began a chemical study of the tartrates, in which he discovered "molecular dissymmetry"—evidenced in this case by a living microorganism, a ferment comparable to yeast, which when placed in a solution of paratartrate of ammonia would select only the "right-handed" tartrates for food, leaving the "left-handed" ones alone. The tartrate study naturally led to an interest in fermentation.

In 1854, when he was only thirty-two years old, Pasteur accepted the position of dean of the university at Lille. Lille was the richest industrial center in the north of France, and once a week Pasteur lectured on some aspect of local industrial production before conducting a tour of the factory concerned. Thus it was that he happened to examine, at a neighboring brewery, the vats in which beet-root juice was fermented into alcohol, one of the region's primary sources of revenue. In samples taken from the vats, he observed uniform microorganisms in the shape of globules, growing and multiplying. He was convinced that these tiny cells, reproducing by sprouting buds, were the secret to fermentation.

But if so, where did these microorganisms come

from? Did they form spontaneously or did they come from "parent" germs? Pasteur favored the latter theory. Proponents of spontaneous generation argued that if his theory were correct, normal air would be a dense fog of reproducing germs. Determined to solve the question once and for all, Pasteur opened some of his little bulbs of sterilized yeast water in the dust-polluted courtyard of the Paris Conservatory; the bulbs all clouded up. But the ones he carried to the top of Mont Blanc (6,500 feet high) remained clear. He thus demonstrated that germs are not evenly distributed in the atmosphere, and that certain areas are almost germ-free.

Pouchet, director of the Museum of Natural History at Rouen, supported the spontaneous generation theory. This formidable adversary was so competitive that he climbed some four thousand feet higher than Pasteur to conduct his experiments. A national dispute arose. When Pasteur held a symposium on the subject at the Sorbonne on April 7, 1864, his audience included Alexandre Dumas père, George Sand, and Princess Matilde. His conclusion was that microscopic beings have never been known to come into the world except from parents resembling them—a conclusion borne out by a commission of the Academy of Sciences. Later Pasteur also advanced the revolutionary theory that fermentations take place in an airless environment; that the microorganisms consume the oxygen available to them and thus gradually decompose.

When he was thirty-five, Pasteur became Administrator of the École Normale and director of its science department. It was an excellent position for one so young, but the buildings were already over-crowded, and Pasteur was forced to set up his laboratory in a couple of attic rooms that were dark in winter and unbearably hot in summer. Perhaps this was one of the reasons that in 1863 and 1864 Pasteur conducted a series of experiments in an old cafe, not far from his father's house in Arbois. The cafe sign was left in the window, but a thirsty traveler would have found only strange-looking equipment on the tables and test tubes in place of wine bottles. Conditions were primitive: heat was supplied by a charcoal brazier, water came from the public fountain in the square, and all utensils were cleaned in the river. Here Pasteur demonstrated that when crushed grapes were deposited in casks for fermentation, they were covered not only with the wild yeasts that convert grape sugar into alcohol, but also with harmful bacteria. Once the wine was bottled, these harmful bacteria often acted up and caused "diseases" of the wine. But Pasteur further demonstrated that these diseases could be prevented entirely simply by heating the wine for several minutes at 55 degrees centigrade (131 degrees Fahrenheit). When connoisseurs protested that heating would change the taste, a conference of professional wine-tasters was called. Between November 16 and November 23, 1865, they sampled twenty-one wines of varying vintages and were forced to admit that the differences between the heated and the unheated wines were so slight as to have escaped nine of the ten experts entirely.

Thus was born the process of pasteurization, which

only later was applied to milk to prevent such infectious diseases as Malta fever (brucellosis) and bovine tuberculosis.

No sooner had Pasteur aided the wine industry than he was called upon to apply his talents to the ailing silkworm industry. For fifteen years silkworm disease had been raging in southern France, accounting for losses of hundreds of millions of francs. Pasteur established his headquarters near a silkworm nursery outside Alès. When he placed the sick silkworms under his microscope, he soon saw that they were covered with small corpuscles. His solution was to insure healthy seed by breeding only from moths without corpuscles. His laboratory method involved isolating every female moth until it began laying, after which it was crushed and examined under the microscope. If it was corpuscular, the seed was destroyed. It was with difficulty that Pasteur persuaded breeders to adopt his method, but when they did the silk industries of southern Europe and Asia Minor were saved. Almost more important than the practical consequences, however, were the pathological considerations: for the first time disease in living creatures had been traced to a microbe. In this little laboratory at Alès, Pasteur examined chrysalises and moths from growers all over southern France to detect the presence of corpuscles. His ability to predict accurately and well in advance whether or not a man's crop would succeed gave him the credentials of a prophet among the growers.

In the fall of 1868 Pasteur had a stroke that left his left side paralyzed. For a while he was convinced that he would never again work independently. "After all," he wrote to a colleague, "what can one do with only one good hand and a sick brain?" Pasteur regained partial use of his leg, but his left arm was lost to him for the rest of his life. Despite this, he attempted to enlist in the Imperial Guard when France and Germany declared war in 1870. And when Paris was besieged and the Museum of Natural History bombarded, Pasteur indignantly returned his honorary doctor's diploma that he had received from Bonn University.

So determined was he to do his part in aiding France against Germany that he decided to study the fermentation of beer and produce a French product superior to the German. His studies soon showed that as in wine, spoilage of beer could be prevented by "pasteurizing" it.

With his reinvolvement in fermentation, Pasteur again became interested in contagious diseases. If fermentation was caused by microorganisms, Pasteur reasoned, might not the deterioration of the body tissues from disease be caused in the same way? "No," answered the traditional physicians in the bitter national feud that followed, "the diseases are within us. Our organisms produce them."

"You are wrong," retorted Pasteur. "The diseases are not already within us; they originate from germs that enter our bodies from outside. As with fermentation, contagious diseases are caused by living agents."

Pasteur had been elected to the Academy of Medicine (he had long been a member of the Academy of

Science) by a single vote. Early in 1874 he surprised the surgeon members of that august body by strongly suggesting that they operate only with instruments that had been passed through boiling water, or better yet, a flame. He was vigorously attacked by traditionalists and skeptics alike. Then Pasteur suddenly decided that France would benefit from having scientists in the Senate, and he announced his candidacy in the Jura district. But practiced as he was at defending his scientific theories, he failed miserably when facing his opponents in the political arena. The rank and file, he discovered, were not particularly attracted by the notion of science represented "in all its purity, dignity, and independence in the Senate," and on election day Pasteur ran far behind his four opponents. It was his single foray into politics.

At the age of fifty-five, Pasteur embarked on a study of contagious diseases. He did so with some misgivings, because he was not a physician. As his first target he selected anthrax, the plague that killed thousands of sheep and cattle all over Europe each year. Microscopic rods, or "bacteridium," had already been discovered in the blood of animals that had died from the disease; Pasteur hypothesized that these microorganisms were the cause of the disease. To prove it he allowed a culture to stand until the microorganisms had settled to the bottom of the test tube. When he injected healthy animals with the solution at the top of the tube, they remained healthy, but when he injected them with the solution at the bottom, they contracted anthrax and died. This experiment was new proof of the germ theory of disease.

Other discoveries followed in rapid succession. In 1879 Pasteur identified a living microorganism as the cause of boils and of osteomyelitis. He named it staphylococcus, or "bunch of grapes," because it never appeared singly but always in a cluster. He also identified another microbe—streptococcus, or "string of beads"—as the cause of the dreaded puerperal sepsis, or "childbirth fever." After his first visit to a maternity ward, he strongly criticized the methods he saw practiced there; to the amazement of the doctors he insisted that the linen used for bandaging should first be sterilized in an oven!

Nearly a century had passed since Edward Jenner first vaccinated against smallpox, and now Pasteur, having isolated the viruses responsible for some diseases, pondered how these viruses might be used to create an immunity to the disease itself. He reasoned that if the cowpox vaccine was simply a weakened form of the smallpox virus, it should be possible to produce an attenuated virus for every contagious disease, which when injected would protect against the disease. After many experiments it was the negligence of his assistants that provided Pasteur with the clue. He was studying the chicken cholera that raged in the barnyards of France. His assistants went off on holiday, and on their return they injected a hen with some old culture that they had prepared before they left. Not only did the fowl not die, but it continued to live after having been injected later with a fresh cholera culture. Pasteur saw the correlation immediately—the first vaccine, sufficiently weakened with age; had immunized the hen. The problem of chicken cholera resolved, Pasteur turned to anthrax. Anthrax germs produced spores that were resistant to aging, and it was only after he had developed a form of the virus without spores by cultivating the "bacteridia" at a temperature of 107 to 109 degrees Fahrenheit that Pasteur was able to produce a vaccine.

The famous test of the anthrax vaccine took place in May, 1881, when Pasteur vaccinated twenty-five sheep in a field at Melun. Two weeks later they and twenty-five unvaccinated sheep were injected with the virulent anthrax "bacteridium" while veterinarians and spectators from all over France looked on. The day after the injections all the unvaccinated sheep were dead, and all the vaccinated ones were healthy. The public was convinced; Pasteur had gambled his whole germ theory on this experiment, and he had won.

Pasteur's research on rabies began as early as 1880, but progress proved difficult because no microbe could be discovered. Starting with the spinal fluid from a mad dog, Pasteur was at last able to weaken the virulence of the virus by injecting it into a series of monkeys. Spinal fluid taken from the last monkey was sufficiently attenuated to be used as a vaccine to immunize dogs against hydrophobia. Thus a vaccine against a contagious disease could be developed even though the microbe itself had never been seen.

But the crucial test of the vaccine against hydrophobia would be its trial on a human being who had been bitten by a mad dog. Pasteur was so confident of its effectiveness that he had almost decided to have himself bitten and try out the vaccine on himself. But fate intervened. Into his laboratory one summer morning walked a nine-year-old boy, Joseph Meister, who had been cruelly bitten by a rabid dog. Pasteur hesitated. Could he make a child his guinea pig? Yet the boy would certainly die otherwise. Thus it was that exactly sixty hours after he had been bitten, Joseph Meister was inoculated under the skin of the abdomen with a small amount of the attenuated virus of rabies. Once and sometimes twice a day the boy was given inoculations of increasingly virulent vaccine. Although Joseph Meister remained healthy and slept peacefully at night, Pasteur himself was pursued by nightmares. But four months later Pasteur was able to report to the Academy of Medicine that the patient was still well.

From all over France people who had been bitten by mad dogs began to pour into Pasteur's laboratory. Injections were given every morning at eleven with Pasteur himself calling out the names and supervising the doses. There was only one death—a ten-year-old girl who had been bitten thirty-seven days before her treatment began. Four little American children even came to Pasteur from New York. They had all recently been bitten by mad dogs, and as they were from workers' families and could not afford the trip, the New York *Herald* had appealed for funds for their journey. When weeks later they sailed home safe and sound, a cheering crowd welcomed them at New York harbor.

Throughout his career Pasteur suffered the calumnies and slanders of other scientists and of the press. The former he answered from the rostrum of the

Academy of Science or the Academy of Medicine; he did his best to ignore the latter. Once he was even challenged to a duel. But his supporters came to far outnumber his critics, and when funds were requested from the public to build the Pasteur Institute in 1886, money poured in from all over France. Pasteur served as the Institute's director until several years before his death, in 1895.

To the end he continued to follow his accustomed routine. "Your father, always very busy, talks little, sleeps little, in other words continues the life that I started with him thirty-five years ago," wrote Madame Pasteur to her son-in-law in 1884. As Pasteur himself put it, "I would feel that I had been stealing if I were to spend a single day without working."

Philip of Macedonia

philippic (fĭ-lĭp′ĭk) *n.* Any verbal denunciation characterized by invective.

When he was fifteen, Philip of Macedonia, the younger brother of King Perdiccas, was taken to Thebes as a hostage to insure the continued good behavior of the Macedonians. Two things about Thebes impressed Philip: the emphasis on organization and tactics within the army; and the love of Hellenic culture among the people, who, unlike their less civilized Macedonian neighbors, did not regard music, art, and drama as degenerate. Thus when Perdiccas died some eight years later and Philip came to the throne (which to all intents and purposes he seized from his infant nephew), his first concerns were to reorganize the army and introduce the nobler achievements of Hellenic culture.

Beginning with a cavalry made up of feuding aristocrats and an ill-organized mass of infantry, Philip molded them into the finest army of ancient times. He insured the loyalty of the nobility by attaching them to himself as personal attendants, retaining the old cavalry term "Companions," but seeing to it that the young nobles were his companions in fact as well as in name. The infantry were divided into many separate mobile units and were designated "Foot Companions"—a term that gave them a new status in which they could take pride. Unlike the armies of the other Greek states, which were generally active only in the regular campaigning season (much as a modern National Guard unit goes to summer camp), Philip's army was constantly at work making conquests. Athens observed all this activity from afar, preoccupied as she was with the conflicts Mausolus had stirred up with her allies (see *mausoleum*), and anxious to believe that Philip's intentions were honorable.

Philip's honor remained to be tested, but his practicality was never in doubt. His early campaign in Thrace brought him a large gold mine with which to finance his ventures and an immense forest to provide timber for his ships. Such conquests, along with the birth of his son, Alexander, and the victory of his horse at Olympia, were reason enough for celebrating the third anniversary of his accession to the throne. By the sixth year of his reign he had lost an eye, but he controlled the entire Thracian coast from Mount Olympus to the mouth of the Nestus. During his tenth year as king, he led his forces in the Sacred War against the sacrilegious Phocians, decorated his victorious troops with laurel as champions of the injured god of Delphi, and had three thousand prisoners thrown into the sea on the pretext that they were impious.

Thus the civilized Athenians already had reason to doubt the peaceful intentions of their neighbor to the north when Philip's ships began to interfere seriously with their own trade routes. Merchant ships carrying grain were captured, and Athenian citizens were taken prisoner; not even a state galley on its way to a religious festival was exempt. In Athens, an anti-Philip party was quickly growing under the leadership of the incomparable orator Demosthenes. An expert lawyer, Demosthenes turned politician when he delivered his First Philippic, an impassioned appeal to the Athenians to realize their danger from Philip and to counteract that danger by creating a standing naval and military force. In this first of his three famous Philippic orations, Demosthenes presented proposals that, had the Athenians taken heed and followed them at once, might have saved Athens and Greece.

But the average Athenian was not ready to divert his beloved festival funds to military uses, as Demosthenes had suggested, and Philip was allowed to go unchecked. He annexed the Chalcidice towns one by one; after the ancient city of Olynthus capitulated, Philip sold the inhabitants into slavery and held a festival in Macedonia with games, dramatic performances, and feasting to celebrate his victories. At last galvanized into action, Athens sent a delegation of ten ambassadors, Demosthenes among them, to contract a peace treaty with Philip. Under the terms of the proposed treaty each party would retain the lands possessed at the time of the ratification. But while the ambassadors were en route, the wily Philip added more Thracian territory to his dominions. When the Greek envoys finally arrived, Philip sent them back to Athens with a letter saying that he would do anything he could honorably do to satisfy the Athenians, although it was clear that he had no intention of altering his plan of conquest. When Demosthenes rose in the Assembly to express his doubts as to the letter's credibility, he was refused a hearing. He was vindicated a few days later when it became known in Athens that Thermopylae had fallen to Philip.

Thus by the thirteenth year of his reign Philip was by far the most powerful man in the Greek world. Macedonia had the advantage of a central government under the personal control of one strong man; Athens, on the other hand, was governed by discussion, and its policies fluctuated on every matter except that the festival money was inviolate. Its army of mercenaries, moreover, was woefully unequal to the immeasurably more efficient Macedonian forces. But a peace treaty was finally ratified, and Philip settled down to Hellenize his kingdom. He invited the most eminent of Greek poets and artists to his court and appointed Aristotle as tutor to Alexander.

The states of the Peloponnese rivaled each other in courting Philip. The Arcadians erected a bronze statue of him at Megalopolis, and Argos voted him a golden crown. But in Athens the mood was becoming increasingly hostile. Demosthenes delivered the Second Philippic—an attempt to prove that Philip was wooing the Peloponnesians and Thebans with a view to isolating Athens and ultimately subjecting her. The Third Philippic, generally considered the greatest of all Demosthenes' speeches, so alarmed the Athenians that they at last agreed to forego the festival money, which was then diverted into the coffers of the military. Demosthenes, by the way, was not above his own form of cruelty. When a messenger arrived in Athens on an errand from Phillip's wife Olympias, Demosthenes had the man arrested as a spy, tortured, and executed. But the people were behind their silver-tongued leader and they publicly crowned him at the festival of Dionysus.

Philip, returning to his campaigns, sailed up the Hellespont. He besieged Byzantium for an entire winter before making a moonlight assault on the town. But the barking of the dogs betrayed him, and he was forced to retire. He suffered another setback when returning from his expedition against the Scythians with his vast numbers of captured slaves and livestock. The Triballi, a wild Balkan people, attacked him, relieved him of his booty, and inflicted great losses on his troops.

Undaunted, Philip returned to Macedonia and at long last turned his attention to the south. Wishing to be sure of Thebes before attacking Athens, he sent ambassadors demanding that the Thebans march with him on Athens or at least allow him free passage through Boetia. But Demosthenes also went to Thebes. Aware of Philip's proposals, he stood before the Theban Assembly and offered terms more generous than his countrymen would even have considered a short time before. He proposed that Thebes and Athens stand together against Philip—Thebes to command at sea, Athens on land. Athens, however, would pay two thirds of the cost of the war. Demosthenes' eloquence was too much for Philip's ambassadors, and Thebes cast her lot with Athens.

She was to suffer for it. The crafty Philip, having prepared his troops to his satisfaction, wrote a letter to one of his generals saying that he must return at once to Thrace to crush a revolt there. The letter fell—not by accident—into Greek hands, and the Greek armies, believing themselves reprieved, relaxed their vigilance. Then, without warning, Philip pounced, inflicting a severe defeat on the Greeks and forcing them to draw up a new line of defense on the plain of Chaeronea.

Several months passed before the two armies again faced each other in battle. Between thirty and thirty-five thousand men were engaged on each side. Alexander, now eighteen years old and no doubt anxious to prove himself in the presence of his father, commanded the left flank, where the best of the professional Macedonian troops opposed the Theban army. Philip commanded the right flank, facing the virtually untrained citizens of Athens. When the battle began, Philip intentionally gave way, drawing the Athenians out of their favored position. Then he suddenly turned on them with his full strength. Those who could (Demosthenes among them), escaped, but a thousand Athenians were killed and two thousand captured. Alexander on his side had more difficulty overcoming the Thebans, who were better soldiers than their allies. The "Sacred Band" of Thebans stood their ground till the last man had fallen. There is today a great mound on the plain of Chaeronea where the Macedonian dead were buried.

Athens prepared at once for the expected siege, but Philip had other plans. To complete the Hellenization of his kingdom, he had to leave Athens intact. Consequently, the terms of the peace he dictated were most generous. Athens was not to be invaded. She was, of course, to become his ally rather than his enemy, and as a proof of his good faith, he sent Alexander to Athens bearing the bones of the Athenians who had died at Chaeronea so that they might be buried in their native soil. In return Philip and Alexander were granted Athenian citizenship, and Philip's statue was erected in the marketplace. But it was all lip service, and in their hearts the people were still at one with Demosthenes. It was he who was chosen to deliver the funeral oration over those who had died at Chaeronea.

Philip was true to his word, however. Inside a year he had welded the Hellenic states into a political and military unit. He needed them united behind him, for he had his eye on Persia, the biggest prize.

But a woman intervened. Olympias, the mother of Alexander, had long before abandoned Philip to the five or six wives who followed her (polygamy was common practice in Macedonia) and had returned to her brother, Alexander of Epirus. Afraid that they might be plotting against him, Philip offered Cleopatra, his daughter by Olympias, to her uncle in marriage. A magnificent celebration was planned. On the appointed day, a statue of Philip was carried into the theater right along with the statues of the gods. Philip himself, supremely confident, walked well ahead of his guards. It was a fatal miscalculation. He was struck down by one of his own men, probably on orders from Olympias.

pickle (pĭk′əl) *n.* Any edible product, such as a cucumber, that has been preserved and flavored in a solution of brine or vinegar. — *tr. v.* To preserve or flavor in a solution of brine or vinegar.

William Beukel (or Beukelz) pickled the first fish in fourteenth-century Holland. Cucumbers came later.

pinchbeck (pĭnch'bĕk') *n.* 1. An alloy of zinc and copper used as imitation gold. 2. A cheap imitation. —*adj.* 1. Made of pinchbeck. 2. Imitation; spurious.

Christopher Pinchbeck, inventor and maker of the famous astronomico-musical clocks, is removed . . . to the sign of the "Astronomico-Musical Clock" in Fleet Street, near the Leg Tavern. He maketh and selleth watches of all sorts, and clocks, as well plain, for the exact indication of time only, as astronomical, for showing the various motions and phenomena of planets and fixed stars.

So read the announcement in *Applebee's Weekly Journal* of July 8, 1721. Not mentioned is the fact that Mr. Pinchbeck invented not only his clocks and watches but the material from which he made them— an alloy of copper and zinc which resembled gold, at least when new. Mechanical singing birds and barrel-organs were also among the products that he exhibited at village fairs under a sign reading "Temple of the Muses."

Samuel Plimsoll

plimsoll (plĭm′səl, -sôl′) *n.* Also **plimsol, plim-sole.** *British.* A rubber-soled cloth shoe; sneaker. [Probably because its mudguard resembles a Plimsoll mark.]

Oh! my God, my God! What can I say, what can I write, to make the people take thought on this terrible wrong?" lamented Samuel Plimsoll of the seaman's lot during Queen Victoria's time. It was not easy to confront people with disagreeable facts in the 1870's —Victoria was on her throne, and all was right with the world. When a ship was lost at sea, as many were at that time, the average Britisher preferred to consider it an act of God; he did not really want to know how many vessels left British ports overloaded, undermanned, and carrying enormous insurance policies. But Samuel Plimsoll was determined that he should hear.

Plimsoll was managing a brewery when he first became interested in maritime affairs. Elected to Parliament from Derby, he was concerned that his tenure not be wasted, and he cast about for a mission that would both satisfy his religious zeal and make him famous. He knew little about shipping, but that did not deter him—the important thing was to choose one's cause, and then master the details. The plight of the British seaman became Plimsoll's cause.

The M.P. from Derby began to haunt the dockyards. He talked with everyone from shipowners and harbormasters to stevedores, sailors, and sailors' widows. Every hardship suffered by the seamen, every unfavorable comment about shipping, was carefully noted. But Plimsoll was after drama, not statistics. What sailor would not, with so avid a listener, embellish his tale? What widow, with so sympathetic an ear, would not dwell on the wrongs that fate had dealt her? Unfortunately, the point at which fact ended and fancy began was lost on Plimsoll.

With the publication of *Our Seamen,* a selection of the most heartrending of the dockyard stories coupled with attacks on everyone from underwriters to shipowning M.P.'s, Plimsoll sparked a virtual explosion of popular anger. Everyone who had been saying for years that something really should be done now agreed that something absolutely had to be done immediately. Although he was justifiably sued for libel by certain shipowners in Parliament and forced to apologize to the House for printing private conversations that had taken place in the sacred grounds of the Commons, Plimsoll achieved his purpose. Numerous acts amending the shipping laws were passed by Parliament and one of them was given his name. The "Plimsoll mark" is an arbitrary line drawn on the hull of a ship beyond which a vessel may not load. That it was made a legal requirement checked the unscrupulous shipowner and greatly diminished the risk faced by the common sailor.

In his later years Plimsoll became concerned about

the extent of ill feeling between England and America. Convinced that the history books used in American schools were the chief culprit, Plimsoll came to America to tackle his new reform, but his health failed him, and he died shortly after returning to England.

poinsettia (poin-sĕt′ē-ə) *n.* A tropical American shrub, *Euphorbia pulcherrima,* having showy, usually scarlet bracts beneath the small yellow flowers.

Joel Roberts Poinsett was a nineteenth-century American romantic, a republican with a small "r," who when sent to represent his government in Buenos Aires, Chile, and later Mexico, could not resist encouraging whatever forces of revolution he encountered. For this he was labeled (by the British) the "most suspicious character" the United States had in South America and the "scourge of the American continent."

Young Joel Poinsett of Charleston, South Carolina, studied medicine but gave it up because of his health; studied law but gave it up because it was too dry; studied military affairs but gave it up because his father opposed it. Then, fluent in many languages but apparently trained for nothing, he obtained his father's consent—and money—for a tour of Europe that lasted seven years.

In St. Petersburg the czar received him after the daily military maneuvers, invited him to the palace for dinner, and sent him on a fact-finding tour of southern Russia. The party consisted of Poinsett, a young English nobleman friend, and seven servants. In the Caucasus they were joined by a Persian merchant with a caravan of covered, latticed carts full of girls destined for the Baku market and Turkish harems. In the Kuban they dined magnificently with the Khan while being entertained by pantaloon-clad girls (whom the Khan much regretted could not be lent to his visitors, as the latter were deemed heretics). The journey could not have been all fun and games, however, as only three of the original party returned alive. His assignment completed, Poinsett turned down a colonelcy in the Russian army in order to continue his odyssey.

At Königsberg he paid a call on the King and Queen of Prussia and heard the beautiful Louise describe how she had pleaded the cause of her country before Napoleon. He met the French emperor in Paris and was present in court on the day when Napoleon rebuked Metternich because the Austrians were arming. Certain that war between Great Britain and America was imminent, Poinsett took ship for home. But the year was 1808, war did not come, and Poinsett suddenly found himself on his way to South American on a semisecret government trade mission.

As consul general for Buenos Aires, Chile, and Peru, Poinsett ignored his country's policy of neutrality in the quarrel between Spain and her colonies. Indeed, he appears to have spent as much time fostering insurrections as concluding trade agreements. In Chile he became a close friend of José Miguel Carrera, the leader of a *junta* that advocated Chilean independence from the viceroy in Peru. The commission formed to draft a constitution met regularly at the American consul general's house, and when the Chilean insurgents clashed with the royalists from Lima, Poinsett accompanied and advised them. Unfortunately, when Carrera was captured and the Chileans were defeated by the Peruvians, Poinsett was held responsible and became persona non grata. The British declared that he was "contaminating the whole population on that side of the continent" and sent a warship to "counteract" the work of "Mr. Poinsett." England and America were finally at war, which cut off Poinsett's direct retreat by sea. So he crossed the Andes to Buenos Aires and from there proceeded to the United States, arriving in Charleston thirteen months later.

Somewhat subdued, Poinsett served quietly in the South Carolina legislature and in Congress for the next ten years. Then in 1825 he was appointed the first American minister to Mexico. Older but apparently no wiser, Poinsett again immediately became embroiled in local politics. Commercial affairs and important negotiations concerning Cuba and Texas took second place to an unending contest for prestige with the British minister. Each would give banquets to which the other was not invited and would use the occasions to disparage the other's government. Since the British minister was in with the "ins," Poinsett devoted his energies to being in with the "outs," naturally earning the fervid animosity of the ruling party. He was accused of promoting internecine strife in order to weaken Mexico; his government was roundly denounced; and his recall was demanded.

Even after a popular revolt brought the republicans into power, the new president of Mexico was forced to send a tactful letter to President Jackson informing him that they really didn't want Poinsett either, and would the president please send a replacement. Still it was this venture that made "Poinsett" a household word, for it was from Mexico that he brought back to South Carolina the Christmas flower that has borne his name ever since.

It would be pleasant to leave Poinsett here, but it is only fair to the honor of Sequoyah and the Cherokees (see *sequoia*) to note that in his last government post, as Secretary of War under President Van Buren, it was Poinsett who effected the transfer (at gunpoint) across the Mississippi of more Indians than had any other war secretary. Although more than twenty thousand Cherokees were peaceably removed (as he proudly pointed out), some four thousand of them died in the process. His father had no doubt been quite right to oppose his entry into military affairs.

Marquise de Pompadour

pompadour (pŏm′pə-dôr′, -dōr′) *n.* 1. A woman's hair style formed by sweeping the hair straight up from the forehead. 2. A man's hair style with the hair brushed up from the forehead.

The King has many trials. People are not sorry enough for him and though he is loved, he is not loved enough. Come, come, Messieurs les Parisiens, may God preserve him for you and also Madame de Pompadour. She has never done anything but good and you are not grateful.

So wrote Voltaire of Louis XV and his mistress toward the end of the Seven Years' War and not long before her death. It was not a disinterested assessment on his part. He had known her for some twenty years—longer even than the king—from the days when still in her teens she was the newly married Madame d' Etioles, determined to have a salon and entertain the intellectuals of her day. The *philosophes* had quite taken her up, for she was as intelligent and talented as she was beautiful, and Voltaire had adopted an almost proprietory attitude toward her. He had been delighted when the king had chosen her for his new favorite, and had written a poem to celebrate the day she was made the Marquise de Pompadour. In her turn she had procured a post and pension for him at Versailles and that most sought after of all favors—a room in the palace itself.

It was only one of the many plums that she, as royal favorite, could bestow. Madame de Pompadour had very real power and at least until the advent of the Seven Years' War, she also had an almost unlimited amount of money to spend as she pleased. On the other hand, a royal mistress could not expect continued loyalty from the king after the initial novelty had worn off: the queen was always there to be reckoned with, and so were scheming, jealous courtiers. If Madame de Pompadour spent many nights poring over reports with the head of the Paris police, it was no sign of paranoia but a sound precaution for someone in her position. Madame de Pompadour was in a less enviable position than most royal mistresses. She was hated by the populace because she had been one of them and had made the leap to the aristocracy, and she was hated by the aristocracy for being a bourgeoise who had elbowed her way into their ranks. For centuries the kings of France had chosen their mistresses from the nobility; indeed, it was an accepted belief that only someone brought up to the intricacies of life at court could possibly carry off so delicate a role. But Madame de Pompadour was ambitious, courageous, and secure in the knowledge that the king was very much in love with her. Moreover, she believed she was fulfilling her destiny.

Jeanne-Antoinette Poisson was the only daughter of an entrepreneur in the food market who was not above making the occasional shady deal, and of a mother who was more admired for her beauty than for her virtue. When she was nine years old, Jeanne had visited a fortune teller, a certain Madame Lebon, who had predicted that she would one day become the mistress of Louis XV. There are indications that not only she, but also her parents, really believed this would happen. Certainly her education and training were far from normal: when she completed convent school at Pouissy and returned to Paris, her parents engaged the best singing, dancing, and deportment masters, and she was tutored in dramatic art and elocution by the eminent Crébillon himself. She could recite entire plays by heart, draw, paint, engrave on precious stones, and play the clavichord superbly. But finding her a suitably distinguished husband was made difficult by the fact that the Poissons were not the sort of people families of distinction generally wanted as relatives. Madame Poisson's lover and protector came to the rescue. By providing the girl with an enormous dowry and the promise of a large inheritance, he managed to persuade his nephew, Charles Guillaume Lenormant d'Etioles, son of the Treasurer of the Mint and a member of an ancient and noble family, to consider marrying her. An hour with the lovely Jeanne-Antoinette was enough. The unfortunate young man fell violently in love, and the match was made.

At Etioles the new young wife divided her time among acting in the theater her husband had built especially for her, playing hostess to the intellectuals and artists of her day, and following the king's hunt in the nearby forest of Senart. This last privilege was one the king accorded to all those living in the neighborhood of his country houses, and young Madame d'Etioles had determined to make the most of it. She drove her phaetons (painted pink and blue to accentuate her own doll-like prettiness) with the same skill that she did everything else, and the king could hardly have helped noticing this vision in pastel that was forever crossing his path. Fortunately for her, the dauphin was being married at just this time, and there were balls almost every night in celebration. The revelers all wore masks, but it soon became noticeable that the king danced almost exclusively with Madame d'Etioles. Two months later she was supping with him at Versailles, and before a third month had passed she had left her grief-stricken husband and moved to apartments at the palace. While he was away with the army, the king provided two courtiers to tutor her in the ways and personages of Versailles, and on his return, having made her a marquise, he stood by in some embarrassment as she was launched into court life with her first curtsy to his long-suffering queen, Marie Leczinska.

The good and devout queen had had to put up with various royal mistresses, and it did not take her long to decide that Madame de Pompadour was a decided improvement over the previous ones. The new favorite was the image of politeness to the queen. She never told nasty stories about her, and she made the king pay her gambling debts. Resigned to the inevitable, the queen was probably quite relieved at her husband's choice and glad not to be responsible for amusing him—a role in which she felt inadequate.

Madame de Pompadour, in her turn, was well aware that keeping the king amused was the key to keeping him at all. To this end she established a tiny theater called the Théâtre des Petits Cabinets with a repertory in which she played all the female leads. While still at Etioles she had become recognized as one of the best amateur actresses in France, and at Versailles her performances were never less than excellent. The Théâtre des Petits Cabinets accommodated only fourteen spectators, and an invitation to a performance soon became one of the most coveted prizes of the court season. However, Madame de Pompadour's fellow Parisians, already at odds with her for defecting from her class, hated her the more for this theater, which they believed to be an unnecessary and immoral extravagance. It was at this time that the first of the hundreds of malicious little anonymous poems and epigrams known as the Poissonades appeared. Composed by courtiers and bourgeois alike, the Poissonades brought much distress to their subject, Madame de Pompadour.

At a dozen odd moments in the day the king, tired from his hunt or bored with his ministers, would run up the secret staircase to the beautiful, warm, scented rooms of his welcoming mistress. Madame de Pompadour would immediately dismiss any visitors (although she had few friends at Versailles, she was constantly besieged by petitioners for favors or advancement) and give the king her undivided attention. Together they would examine the latest works of art that she had commissioned or select fabrics or furniture for the king's private rooms, which they were always redecorating, or they would study plans for the latest in the series of houses they were building or renovating. Madame de Pompadour had three chateaux of her own—besides the Hôtel d'Evreux in Paris, the hermitages at Versailles, Fontainebleau, and Compiegne—that also required attention. She was like a general at the head of a veritable army of architects, builders, painters, sculptors, and gardeners. Fortunately for France, she had impeccable taste. After she acquired her house at Bellevue, the king gave her the whole village of Sèvres, where she established the great national porcelain factories.

Most of all she collected. She could not resist a beautiful object, and hers was the France of elaborate Rococo elegance. After she died, the sale of her collections continued for eight months. At Versailles she lived amid a profusion of gilt carving and mirrors, which reflected the light of elaborate chandeliers hung from ceilings frescoed with Venuses. One can imagine her there, as radiant and beautiful as her surroundings, her golden hair dressed well back from her brow in the fashion that still carries her name.

But time passes, even for the lovely mistresses of kings, and Madame de Pompadour's role altered with it. The Théâtre des Petits Cabinets was given up after five years; by the end of the seventh year, the secret staircase to the king's chambers had been boarded up. Her hours of play and of idle, gossipy talk gave way to hours in Council and discussions with ambassadors and ministers, for the king put great trust in her judgment and always consulted her before acting on any issue of importance. Just as she had once worked tirelessly to amuse him, so she labored now to make herself politically indispensable to him. Her big moment came when the king asked her to meet the Austrian ambassador and negotiate an alliance between France and Maria Theresa's Empire. The secret session took place at her little summerhouse under the terrace at Bellevue. She believed herself fully knowledgeable in European politics and was delighted by the chance to play an important diplomatic role. Kaunitz, the ambassador, was a skilled negotiator, but Madame de Pompadour made up for her lack of experience by her cleverness. The terms of the ensuing treaty were not at all disadvantageous to France. However, Austria was France's traditional enemy, and the people and the generals hated the alliance. Fighting broke out, and after a few early victories, France suffered a whole series of reversals. Not the generals, nor the army, but Madame de Pompadour was blamed.

During the seven long years of the war, the king moved his office into his mistress' red lacquered room. It became headquarters where ministers were received and state papers lodged. The marquise was consulted on all matters and advised about everything. She even outlined military strategy to Marshal d'Estrées (on her fan, as the story goes). In public she maintained the cheerful assurance of a true diplomat, but in private she worried over the war's course and brooded over each defeat. The natural finale to her fairy-tale life would have been for France to win great victories and for the king to emerge covered with glory, his faithful adviser and helpmate at his side. Instead the war brought ruin and humiliation to France, scorn to her king, and increased animosity toward his mistress, Madame de Pompadour.

In 1764, at the official opening of the Place de la Concorde, built to celebrate the peace that finally did come, Madame de Pompadour gave a splendid fireworks display. It was the last time the people saw her. She became ill soon afterward at her favorite estate, Choisy. The king, however, could not bear to leave her, and in spite of the ruling that only royalty might die at Versailles, he took her back there. He was in his mid-fifties, she in her early forties, and they had been together for almost twenty years. She had survived more than one attempt by beautiful and titled ladies to unseat her; she had also survived the hatred of certain ministers and the unceasing opposition of the Church. Once when Louis had lain critically wounded from an assassin's attack, she had packed her bags to leave Versailles, but Louis had recovered and she had unpacked them. Her health had never been good — she had suffered many miscarriages in her efforts to bear him a child — and the strain of the war had told more on her than on him. She was tubercular and anemic; perhaps most of all simply exhausted. Her beauty was gone, but her courage never left her. On her last day she painted her face with care, bade farewell to the king, and called for the priest. When she had confessed, the priest turned to go, but she stopped him, saying, "One moment, Monsieur le Curé, we'll go out together," and died.

praline (prä'lēn, prā'-) *n.* A crisp confection made of nut kernels stirred in boiling sugar syrup until brown.

Césair, Comte du Plessis-Praslin, rose in his profession through his family connections and gained immortality because of the inspiration of his chef. A member of one of the oldest families in Champagne, the young count shared schoolbooks with the prince who would become Louis XIII, listened to the royal tutor speak on fortifications and the arts of attack and defense, and at fourteen was put in command of a regiment by his uncle, General Charles de Choiseul. While still in his teens he fought a duel in the Bois de Boulogne with the young Abbé de Gondy (later Cardinal of Retz). Although not only the adversaries but also their seconds were wounded, the affair was successfully hushed up by the count's family.

Under the fond eye of Cardinal Richelieu, the military career of du Plessis-Praslin so prospered that he was made a lieutenant-general. But after Richelieu died, and Cardinal Mazarin succeeded him as chief minister, the count found that his climb to the top had become much steeper. It was only after a good deal of negotiation and counternegotiation, considerable sulking, and another victory in the field that he was made a field marshal. He immediately started agitating for the rank of *duc et pair*. Du Plessis-Praslin took command of the royal army during the revolt of the nobles in 1648–49 and prevented the archduke Leopold, governor general of the Spanish Netherlands, from crossing the frontier into France. He led the French army against Spain in 1650, and three years later was called in to complete a siege that Mazarin himself had commanded until he ran into military problems beyond his scope. After the capitulation was signed, Mazarin and Louis XIV dined at the field marshal's house. Whether or not it was on this occasion that du Plessis-Praslin's chef produced the sugary concoction that carries his name has not been recorded. But we do know that much of the meal was taken up with the host's open hints at his desire for further advancement. Mazarin, however, felt that the young king's enthusiastic praise was quite sufficient reward for anyone.

Meanwhile, du Plessis-Praslin had become "gouverneur" of the king's younger brother—Monsieur, as he was known—and at this point he ended his formal military career in order to devote full time to the young prince's education. After Monsieur married Princess Henrietta of England, du Plessis-Praslin became first gentleman of the bedchamber. But the *duc et pair* still eluded him, and when Louis created fourteen new dukes and he was not one of them, the marshal was so incensed that on the day the new titles were registered, he attended the ceremony, stood behind the last duke, and in spite of the king's attempts at jollying, would not be consoled. He was convinced he would die without the honor he so longed for, but in actual fact it came to him only two years later. Du Plessis-Praslin lived for another decade — at last, it is to be hoped, satisfied.

George M. Pullman

pullman (po͞ol'mən) *n.* A railroad parlor car or sleeping car.

George M. Pullman fulfilled the American dream; he started out in a farm supply store and died a multi-millionaire. Trained as a cabinetmaker, he decided that the sleeping cars of his time could be improved. And indeed, shortly before the outbreak of the Civil War, there was a lot to improve. The typical sleeping car was equipped with a dozen or so bunks attached to one side. Lumpy mattresses lay across them, but amenities such as sheets, pillows, or blankets were nonexistent. The usual practice was to go to bed fully clothed, including one's boots, and hope (in winter) that the little box stove would keep the temperature above freezing. An occasional flickering candle was the only light, and the washing facilities consisted of a communal towel, basin, and pitcher of water.

Pullman and a friend set to work converting two day coaches of the Chicago and Alton Railroad into sleeping cars. Individual "sleeping sections," complete with soft mattresses and warm blankets, were served by two washrooms and lit by oil lamps. On the inaugural trip, the conductor reported some difficulty persuading the passengers to remove their boots, but that proved to be only a matter of educating the public.

Realizing that considerable capital would be needed to continue his improvements, Pullman went west to dig for gold. Although he purportedly failed in his quest, he returned to Chicago with a mysterious twenty thousand dollars to invest in what he felt would be the best sleeping car in history. The Chicago Union Station now stands over the spot where Pullman built the Pioneer. Costing four times as much as his previous cars, it met Victorian standards of roominess so well that it was too high to go under the bridges and too wide to pull up to the platforms. The fate of the car might have remained uncertain but for the lucky accident of President Lincoln's assassination. Both Chicago and Lincoln's burial place, Springfield, were in Illinois, and with the reputation of the state at stake, the Chicago and Alton Railroad altered their platforms and raised their bridges. The funeral party traveled in the Pioneer, which was much admired, and the public demand for similar cars was immediate.

The Pioneer was equipped with lower, new, hinged upper berths. Its interior was luxurious and its mattresses were spread not only with blankets but with sheets as well. It was, in fact, not unlike a hotel on wheels and as such it required servicing like a hotel. So Pullman went into the bedding supply business and was operating forty-eight cars of the Pioneer variety when he joined Andrew Carnegie to form the Pullman Palace Car Company. Travel had become vastly more civilized, but one major detriment remained — the passengers still had to pour off the train three times a day to consume at top speed the generally bad food offered by station restaurants. So Pullman invented his "hotel car," a sleeping car with a small kitchen at one end, which was soon replaced by the Pullman diner. The menu in the 1870's varied from sirloin steak at fifty cents to snipe or quail at seventy-five cents, to the deluxe prairie chicken at one dollar.

When it became apparent that an assembly-line plant was required to meet the demand for Pullman Palace Cars, Pullman purchased thirty-six hundred acres a few miles south of Chicago and prepared to construct an entire town for his employees and their families. According to the initial plans, there was not to be anything paternalistic about it: management was to finance the building costs, but houses were to be rented and services to be charged as in any other community. The town of Pullman was built and before long was inhabited by some twelve thousand people. But it was not all smooth sailing. Rents and gas and water rates were from 10 to 25 per cent higher than in neighboring Chicago and caused the grumbling citizens of Pullman to sue. The courts later required the company to sell all property not actually used for industrial purposes. Although the company prospered to the point where it had a $25 million surplus and had bought out practically all its competitors, it laid off well over half of its employees and then began to rehire them at wage cuts of 20 to 25 per cent. Employees who attempted to discuss the matter with Pullman were fired on the spot, and when arbitration was suggested, Pullman countered by saying: "We have nothing to arbitrate." Later he elaborated: "The workers have nothing to do with the amount of wages they shall receive."

When all Pullman workers struck, and the American Railway Union announced a boycott of all railroads employing Pullman cars, President Cleveland ordered troops into Chicago to enforce a court injunction against the strikers. Twelve men were killed in the riots that followed; the young president of the American Railway Union, Eugene Debs, went to jail; and the strike was broken when a trainload of fresh meat left the stockyards with a cavalry escort on July 10, 1894. Pullman had won, but his tactics have forever tainted his name.

quisling (kwĭz'lĭng) *n.* A traitor who serves as the puppet of the enemy occupying his country.

Vidkun Quisling was, the Germans say, the only man who ever managed to bluff Hitler. The Nasjonal Samling (National Unity) party of Norway, which he had formed in the early 1930's, never attained more than 2.2 per cent of the vote in a general election and had no representatives in the Storting. These were facts that Hitler should have known, even if he was not aware that the Norwegian populace generally had only contempt for Quisling and indeed suspected that he was mentally unbalanced. But Hitler, who evidently met with Quisling in Germany shortly before the invasion of Norway and informed him then of the imminent occupation, appears to have sincerely believed that this was the man who could persuade the Norwegian people to comply more or less happily with their German "protectors."

Hitler was soon to discover that nothing could have been further from the truth. When in the early morning hours of April 9, 1940, German troops occupied Oslo and took over all communications, Norwegians turned on their radios to hear with amazement their own countryman, ex-major Vidkun Quisling, a former military attaché in Petrograd and Helsinki and for two years minister of defense, broadcast his intent to place himself at the service of the invading forces. Furthermore, continued Quisling, because both the king and Parliament had left the capital (they had only just managed to escape), he would personally take over the leadership of the country. He would, in fact, become Norway's new prime minister.

If any Norwegian had been unclear as to what had actually happened, Quisling's broadcast brought the whole situation rapidly into focus. The citizens of Norway were being asked to accept as their leader a man whom all but a few of them found ridiculous. When in the course of the next few days Quisling tried to set up a government, no one would join, nor would anyone in the existing government work with him. He was ignored by everyone in authority—by the chiefs of the government offices, the police, the Oslo civic authorities, and the trade unions. No one except the Führer far away in Germany would back him—but back him the Führer did! Dr. Brauer, the German minister to Norway, who knew well Quisling's standing, had obviously not been consulted. He made a long call to Berlin that afternoon, speaking first to Ribbentrop, then to Hitler himself. Brauer protested, but to no avail—Hitler insisted that Quisling was indeed Prime Minister of Norway.

But even with the assurance of the Führer's support, Quisling found himself in deep trouble. When he dismissed the chief of the Oslo police three days later, the German command quietly told that officer not to take any notice. By April 15 the rage of the Norwegian people had reached such a pitch that open revolution was clearly imminent, and the German authorities gave Quisling exactly one hour (some say ten minutes) to get out of his headquarters in the Continental Hotel. A Council of Administration took over the government.

But Hitler, it appeared, was not to be proved wrong so easily. Quisling remained head of the Nasjonal Samling and bided his time; in August he went to Berlin in an attempt to get rid of those who had gotten rid of him. Time passed; then on February 1, 1942, again over the protestations of the German command in Oslo, Quisling was returned to the premiership. With the official title of Minister-President, he sat on King Haakon's chair in the palace, surrounded by members of the cabinet, stormtroopers, and the Gestapo. He moved into a forty-six-room villa on an island near Oslo, where he had the walls reinforced, a bomb shelter added, and a battery of antiaircraft and machine guns installed. He furnished the interior with paintings from the Oslo museum and ate from dishes of gold and silver, but he was so afraid of poisoning that he had every dish sampled by someone else first. He was accompanied by one hundred and fifty bodyguards wherever he went, and rode in a bullet-proof limousine (a present from Hitler) whose license plate was changed daily.

Five days after he had returned to office, Quisling decreed that all powers formerly held by the king and Parliament were now vested in him, and that his signature would legalize anything, regardless of the

Constitution. He ordered his picture hung in all public buildings and new postage stamps issued with his portrait. Then he went to Berlin to call on the Führer and probably to work out details of the Nazification of Norway and her gradual assimilation into the Third Reich. Quisling's personal goals included taking over Greenland, Iceland, and the Shetland and Faroe Islands, and colonizing North Russia.

In fact, Quisling remained an ineffective administrator and organizer, and the Germans saw to it that actual control of the government never left their hands. Quisling spent his time giving orders to the Hird — young Norwegians who supposedly corresponded to Hitler's SS — but who were actually the pick of the riffraff. Nevertheless, they managed to terrorize whole communities with their brutal acts. As head of the Nasjonal Samling, Quisling had first thought he could coerce the people into joining his party. When that failed, he tried to cajole them into membership with slogans. But the membership, if anything, dropped below its preoccupation level.

Quisling remained premier until the end of the occupation. Hitler must have recognized Quisling's complete ineffectuality long before that time and must have deplored his outspokenness (he very nearly brought on a crisis when he suddenly announced in August, 1943, that Norway was at war with Russia). But as the war went on the German Führer had other more pressing concerns and seems to have been content to let matters rest. When in May, 1945, the Germans in Norway surrendered, Quisling was arrested and taken to Mollergaten No. 19, the prison where he had confined so many of the resistance fighters. There he was left through most of the summer to storm about, complaining bitterly that the accommodations in his cell were not fitting for one of his rank.

His trial opened on August 20, 1945. The charges against him ran from misappropriation of state and personal property to collaborating with a foreign enemy to bring Norway under its power to outright murder. He pleaded "not guilty on any count," but the evidence against him mounted. It included documents from the German archives that proved beyond a doubt that he had provided Hitler with military information on the fortifications of the Oslo Fjord. He was accused of mass murder of Norwegian Jews but denied any knowledge of their deportation. He wrote out a sixty-nine-page document in his defense, but neither judge nor jury was persuaded. Norway's traitor, her quisling, was condemned to death and shot by a firing squad.

raglan (răg'lən) *n.* A loose coat, jacket, or sweater with slanted shoulder seams and with the sleeves extending in one piece to the neckline. — *adj.* Having the shoulder seams slanted and extending to the neckline: *a raglan sleeve.*

On the evening of the Battle of Waterloo, during which he had served as Wellington's principal aide-de-camp, Lord Fitzroy Somerset, aged twenty-three, was hit in the right elbow by a musketball fired by a sniper on a farmhouse roof. He walked back to a cottage that was serving as a hospital and showed the wound to the surgeon in charge, who told him to lie down on the table and proceeded to cut off his arm. Lord Fitzroy made no sound until the surgeon tossed away the limb; then the Prince of Orange, who was lying in the same room, heard him call out, "Here, bring back my arm! The ring my wife gave me is on the finger!"

Such stoic courage remained characteristic of Lord Fitzroy all his life, although he perhaps did not have to call on it again until forty years later, when, having become the first Lord Raglan, he was appointed commander-in-chief of the British Expeditionary Army to the East. During the intervening four decades, when Britain was at peace, he had continued to serve the Duke of Wellington, officially as his military secretary, actually as a kind of alter ego. He functioned as an executor, a diplomatist, and a buffer between the extraordinary Wellington and the outside world.

But in 1852 the old duke died; in 1854 England, uninvolved in the Franco-Russian dispute over the Palestinean holy places but bored with four decades of peace, joined forces with her traditional enemy, France, to declare war against her traditional ally, Russia. Queen Victoria had overcome her doubts about whether England should defend so-called Turkish independence, and less than three weeks later General Lord Raglan set sail for the Crimea as commander-in-chief of the British forces.

At sixty-five Lord Raglan might have been thought overage for active generalship in wartime, but the fact was that of the five British generals commanding infantry divisions only one was under sixty, and the cavalry was not much better off. The real problem was that Raglan had been sitting behind a desk for forty years and had never commanded troops in the field or led them into battle. It would be wrong, however, to assume that the government had erred in its choice. With rare exceptions only the nobility were entitled to high military rank, and of the available nobles, Lord Raglan was almost surely the best man. He inspired great confidence in the populace because of his long association with Wellington, and he spoke excellent French (although he was unfortunately in the habit of forgetting that France was now his ally and kept saying "the French" when he meant "the enemy").

Lord Raglan arrived in the Crimea without any fanfare, wearing the blue frock coat that he always wore and that he continued to wear throughout the campaign. With his rather ascetic face, his civilian clothes, and his extreme modesty, he neither looked nor acted like the commanding general. Many soldiers complained that the commander was never seen with the army merely because they had no idea that the great General Raglan was the simply dressed, unobtrusive man who was always among them. In fact, Raglan's lack of experience with the troops made him uneasy with them, and he was far too shy and modest to enjoy being cheered by his men in the customary British way. But in time he became more used to them, and by the end they loved him dearly.

In defense of Lord Raglan's record in the Crimea it should be noted that he was much handicapped by his joint command with the over-cautious French, by terrible weather conditions, including a tornado and an exceptionally bitter winter, and by phenomenal bungling in England that prevented him from getting the supplies he needed. But in retrospect the allied command probably blundered only slightly less often than the Russians. And unfortunately for Lord Raglan, he was apt to attribute to his generals much more intelligence and foresight than most of them actually possessed. He had been an adviser so long and a leader so briefly.

He was fearless to the point of recklessness. At Alma he rode far ahead of his army, right past the French skirmishers (who were no doubt amazed at the sight of this extraordinary English general in his blue frock coat, white shirt, and black cravat), and on into the Russian lines, where the view happened to be much better. Some days later, while the British army was marching around Sebastopol, the entire cavalry took a wrong turn in the woods and got lost. Lord Raglan, who believed he was following the cavalry when he was actually far ahead of it, suddenly collided with a large body of Russian infantry. He quietly told one of his staff to go find the cavalry; then he reined up and sat facing the enemy so calmly that it never occurred to the confused Russian soldiers that this was the British commander-in-chief, who with his staff had somehow lost the British army and was quite defenseless. Raglan directed the Battle of Balaclava from the heights above the actual fighting, but at Inkerman he occupied a ridge with round shot whistling past and shells exploding throughout, and at Malakoff and Redan he stood in the mortar battery behind the forward trench under heavy fire.

But bravery is not enough in generals. After Alma, Lord Raglan was unable to convince the French of the necessity of marching immediately to Sebastopol. At Balaclava his famous four orders were so ambiguous that they were at least partially to blame for the loss of the Light Brigade. Inkerman was as bloody as it was inconclusive. Raglan's failure to realize the necessity of controlling the Woronzoff Road brought about many of the horrors of the ensuing winter.

Lord Raglan watched his army perish before his eyes during that winter of 1854–55. His men froze to death because the goverment in London refused to believe that a Crimean winter was not balmy; they starved because there was no road by which to transport those supplies that did reach the little harbor at Balaclava. His days were an endless round of orders, dispatches, instructions, and letters to the parents of all the officers who died. Because he rode around the camps as inconspicuously as possible, often after nightfall and always half-concealed in the big-sleeved cloak to which he lent his name, his men believed him aloof and unconcerned with their sufferings. At home he became the target of increasingly bitter attacks, first from *The Times,* then from other newspapers, later in Parliament, and finally — although always privately — from the queen herself. He became the scapegoat (although he never stooped to answer the charges) for the slow progress of the war and the suffering of his troops.

Actually the suffering affected him deeply, and as the winter wore on he spent more and more time with his men, trying to cheer them by his presence. On hearing that the wife of a corporal (many wives had accompanied their husbands, despite the lack of provisions for them) had given birth to a baby girl on the bare ground, he went personally to visit her, riding through a howling wind and kneeling in the snow at the flap of her little tent to talk with her. He did his best to reorganize the outrageously inadequate medical facilities. Florence Nightingale accomplished her miracles at the base hospital in Scutari, but the conditions in the ship and field hospitals at Balaclava remained dreadful throughout the winter. By spring, things were generally improved, and Miss Nightingale found much to praise when she visited in May.

At last, on June 18, the anniversary of Waterloo, an assault was made on Sebastopol. The city was well fortified, the defenders' fire deadly, and after the British troops had given way and the guns at last had stopped, the British losses totaled fifteen hundred men. Pausing after the battle to speak to a wounded officer, Lord Raglan found himself roundly cursed and personally blamed for every drop of blood shed that day. He returned to his headquarters with outward calm, but the inner depression gained ground, and within a week he was dead. There was not, said the doctors, sufficient physical cause—it appeared he had truly died of a broken heart. On the afternoon of July 3, a coffin draped with the Union Jack and a wide-sleeved black cloak was lowered onto the barrel of a nine-pounder. The gun was rolled out of the farmyard where the British had their headquarters and on through the double ranks of infantry down to the sea. It was closely followed by Lord Raglan's favorite horse, Miss Mary, saddled but riderless, and by thousands of soldiers after her. During the ceremony the trenches were left almost empty, but the Russians took no advantage of the situation.

Marquis de Sade

sadism (sā′dĭz′əm) *n.* 1. *Psychology.* The association of sexual satisfaction with the infliction of pain on others. Compare *masochism.* 2. Broadly, delight in cruelty.

Donatien Alphonse François de Sade was a member of the highest nobility. Born in 1740 at the Paris residence of the great Prince de Condé, he was a marquis at birth. At the age of six he was sent by his father, the Comte de Sade, to be educated by his uncle, an abbé, who was at once a noted naturalist, an authority on Petrarch, and a typical wordly priest of his time whose household was run by a charming manageress with the aid of various attractive maids. At ten the boy was removed from this domestic Eden to the more rigid disciplines of a Jesuit school, and at fourteen he was declared by his father to have learned enough and to be ready for the next stage of the normal nobleman's education—the army. There he spent several years in the scarlet, white, and gold of the aristocratic Royal Light Horse Guards, followed by several more years in the scarlet and blue of the equally noble Burgundian Cavalry. The young marquis was handsome, and although only about five feet two inches tall, he looked quite dashing when mounted and on parade. The Comte felt his son had turned out quite well.

But the Marquis de Sade had no interest in soldiering and looked on regimental routine as merely the stage setting for a life of sport and pleasure. The sports and pleasures of the nobility are, however, always expensive, and his son's continuous requests for money became increasingly burdensome to the Comte de Sade, who was much richer in ancestors than he was in francs. His profligate son obviously needed a wife with a sizable dowry. The Comte soon discovered that the President of the Third Chamber of the High Court of Paris, M. de Montreuil, to whom he owed considerable money, had a marriageable daughter. Moreover, Madame de Montreuil, who was only rich bourgeoisie, was most anxious for aristocratic connections. The Comte de Sade and Madame de Montreuil sat down to bargain. The result was that a dowry worth well over half a million dollars would be traded for the title of Marquise. When the young couple met, the prospective bride, Mlle. Renée-Pelagie, found herself much the taller of the two, but she was too much awed by her future husband's courtly manners and unimpeachable pedigree to be anything but delighted. The match pleased everyone but the young marquis, who realized the necessity of marrying money but had hoped to marry charm, wit, and a pretty face as well. Poor Renée had none of these. Still, it was an accepted formula for marriage in the eighteenth century, and no one would have objected if the husband quietly used part of his wife's money to support a few mistresses on the side. What neither the bride nor her mother could ever have foreseen was the extent of the indiscretion and the depth of the debauchery that was to characterize the marquis's life almost from his wedding day.

Would the Marquis de Sade have behaved differently if he could have married whom and when he chose? During his engagement he was seriously involved with another woman — some say it was Renée's younger sister, Anne; others, a certain mysterious Laure de Lauris of Avignon. But whether he was actually in love with either will probably never be known. What is known is that within a few months of his marriage de Sade was arrested by Inspector Marais of the Paris police in one of the *petites maisons* of promiscuity of the countryside around Paris and was taken in a closed carriage to the prison at Vincennes.

The exact charge against de Sade has been lost, but considering the licentiousness of the age and de Sade's noble name, it could hardly have been less than a written description of an unlawful sexual act (such as sodomy) that provided incontrovertible evidence of his having committed the act of which he wrote. After two months confinement, de Sade was released, exiled from Paris, and retired to his chateau of La Coste in Provence. In Renée's absence (she had remained in Paris) he installed one of his old mistresses, entertained lavishly, and instituted a succession of clandestine revels, which concluded only when the king withdrew the sentence of exile and allowed the marquis to return to the capital.

For several years de Sade seems to have managed to keep his affairs out of the public eye; then suddenly he was arrested for assault and torture in what became widely known as the Rose Keller affair. Although he was finally cleared of the charge (the defendant turned out to be a prostitute, and what are a few bruises and scratches to a prostitute if the pay is high enough?), the trial received much publicity. Madame de Montreuil, finding the price of upward mobility higher than she had anticipated, became alarmed. Once again released from prison and exiled from Paris, de Sade returned to La Coste. There he took up his former way of life at an increased tempo, established a season of theatricals in which he played all the principal parts, entertained on an even grander scale, and went heavily into debt.

It was at this point that Anne de Montreuil left her convent and came to La Coste as a companion to her older sister. Anne was as bright, pretty, and daring as Renée was dull, plain, and conventional, and she and de Sade were immediately attracted to each other. What was happening must soon have been clear to everyone at La Coste, including the marquise. The only question is why Madame de Montreuil did not become aware of the situation and remove her younger daughter. But even in this period of real romantic involvement, de Sade could not forego the degenerate pleasures to which he had by now become addicted. He and his valet Latour visited Marseilles, where they reversed their identities and called at a house of prostitution. The events of the afternoon seem to have included flagellation, sodomy, and the passing around of aphrodasiac sweets, which made several of the girls ill and gave rise to the charge (later disproved) that they were poisonous. De Sade and Latour returned to La Coste, but rumors that the girls were pressing charges against them with the Marseilles police caused them to flee to Italy, accompanied by Anne.

Now, Madame de Montreuil might have forgiven her son-in-law for poisoning prostitutes, but she could not forgive him the incestuous seduction of her younger daughter, particularly as it was not only open gossip, but actually hawked about by the news vendors. The honor of her family was now forever besmirched. Determined to get the marquis behind bars once and for all, she seized upon the Marseilles incident, had warrants issued for the arrest of both de Sade and Latour on the charge of attempted murder, packed the court with her friends and agents, and saw to it that the marquis and his valet were convicted of poisoning and sodomy—"the said de Sade to be decapitated on a scaffold . . . and the said Latour, on a gallows, to be hanged by the neck and strangled." In the absence of the living culprits, their effigies were duly executed and burned.

Madame de Montreuil then discovered de Sade's whereabouts in Sardinia and had him arrested and imprisoned there. But Renée turned out to be an unexpected adversary, for she preferred the status quo to revenge and wanted her husband back. The marquise suddenly appeared at the prison gates accompanied by fifteen armed men and somehow effected her husband's escape.

During the next four years that they lived at La Coste, de Sade restricted himself to a succession of young domestics—seamstresses, cooks, and scullery maids—who would invariably quit, attempt to bring allegations against their employer, and be shushed up in turn by the marquise, who likewise thwarted all her mother's attempts to have her husband arrested. Finally de Sade committed the fatal error of returning to Paris, where once again he was arrested by Inspector Marais and taken to the jail at Vincennes.

Thus at the age of thirty-seven, the Marquis de Sade began the long period of imprisonment that, except for one escape and six brief weeks of freedom, continued for the next thirteen years. There was no charge; he was held by *lettre de cachet*—a sort of preventive detention "at the request of his family," meaning Madame de Montreuil, for the loyal Renée never ceased in her efforts to free him. It was at Vincennes, and later in the octagonal tower of the Bastille, that de Sade wrote treatises on sociological and political subjects, on utopias and revolutions, and the famous novels that are the products of a mind obsessed by a ferocious sensuality, which had no natural outlet. *The 120 Days of Sodom,* in which the author lists six hundred variations of the sex instinct, was written in thirty-seven days on a roll of paper thirty-nine feet long. *Justine* was composed in less than half that time.

During the spring of 1789 de Sade became aware that something was happening outside the walls of the Bastille. Eager to become a part of the general unrest, he prepared a number of signs, which he managed surreptitiously to hang over the muzzles of the cannon in plain sight of the people below. The signs proclaimed in large red letters such sentiments as "PEOPLE! COME DESTROY THE TERRIBLE BASTILLE!" and "ARM YOURSELVES, BRAVE FRENCHMEN, COME TO THE AID OF THE VICTIMS OF TYRANNY!" and (ignoring the fact that there were no more than nine prisoners in the Bastille) "FIVE HUNDRED MISERABLE CAPTIVES WILL DIE IF YOU DELAY THEIR RESCUE!" After this escapade the marquis was barred from exercising on the ramparts, but he still could not be silenced. The Bastille logbook contains the following entry for July 2, 1789: "A number of times the Count de Sade shouted from the window that the Bastille prisoners were being slaughtered and would people come and rescue him!" In the early hours of July 4 he was transferred to the Charenton Asylum, and thus he was not in the Bastille ten days later when it was stormed by the revolutionaries seeking the weapons they knew to be stored there.

De Sade remained in Charenton until the spring of 1790, when all *lettres de cachet* prisoners were released. He was fifty, suffering from obesity and rheumatism, and nearly penniless. All his personal property, including a library of six hundred volumes, had gone up in flames in the Bastille; La Coste had been sacked by the local peasantry, and Renée had finally given up, retreated into a nunnery, and filed for a separation order. The marquis settled near the Place Vendôme in Paris with a young actress, Madame Quesnet, whose husband had abandoned her and her child. It was a mutually happy alliance that lasted the rest of his life. He joined the local revolutionary cell and became Citizen Sade, claiming that he had been a victim of the old order and expounding his own social philosophy at every opportunity. In due time he became commissioner of his section and as such managed to have the Montreuils put on the "cleared" list, thus with ironic magnanimity saving his mother-in-law from the guillotine.

In fact, the same de Sade who had been charged with torture and attempted murder, who had stormed about at La Coste and raged from his cell at the Bastille, was a mild, benevolent revolutionary. He managed to save so many of his friends from the guillotine that in December, 1793, he was arrested for "moderantism." In the course of the next few months he was moved from prison to prison until finally he was confined in the Picpus hospital, a relatively pleasant place until the guillotine was set up just below its windows and the dead disposed of in the garden behind. "We buried 1,800 in thirty-five days, one-third being taken from our own unfortunate home," wrote de Sade of this period. On the morning of July 27, 1794, the court bailiff went from prison to prison rounding up a group of accused to bring them to trial. But he could not find de Sade. There had been so many prison transfers that the records were not up to date; the authorities simply did not yet show in their books that de Sade had been moved to the Picpus hospital. That afternoon, Citizen Sade watched the mass execution in which he had been scheduled to die. Then on July 28 Robespierre was guillotined, and the Terror ended.

After the Revolution, de Sade eked out a living as a stage prompter while continuing to publish. After

Napoleon came to power, de Sade circulated a scurrilous little pamphlet with portraits of Napoleon and Josephine and once again was arrested and sent to Charenton, now a lunatic asylum. There he set up his famous theater, drilled the inmates until they became quite acceptable performers, brought in professional actresses from Paris theaters, and invited all his influential friends to attend. In time the lunatic plays at Charenton became quite fashionable.

The first thirteen years of de Sade's imprisonment had come to an end with the Revolution; the second thirteen years culminated in his death. "They could leave me here ten years and they'd take me out no better, believe me, than I was when I went in," de Sade had once written from the Bastille. "Either kill me or accept me as I am, for Devil take me if ever I change—I've told you that the beast's too old."

Just as the guillotine (see *guillotine*) had existed before Guillotin, so sadism existed before de Sade. But a century before Freud, de Sade's life caused people to recognize that in this world there is not only cruelty, but the lust for cruelty; not only destruction, but the desire for destruction. "As for my vices— unrestrainable rages—an extreme tendency in everything to lose control of myself, a disordered imagination in sexual matters such as had never been known in this world, an atheist to the point of fanaticism—in two words, there I am," de Sade once wrote, "and so once again kill me or take me like that, because I shall never change."

Earl of Sandwich

sandwich (sănd′wĭch, săn′-) *n.* Two or more slices of bread with meat, cheese, or other filling placed between them.

There is some difference of opinion as to whether the Earl of Sandwich asked his manservant for a piece of meat between two slices of bread while he was engaged at the writing table or at the gaming table. Those trying to salvage something of his more than slightly tarnished reputation assure us of the former, but the latter makes a better story and has by far the greater number of supporters. No one will ever be certain, for two centuries of sandwich-eating have intervened; moreover, the popular image of an unnoble earl has persisted for so long that the chances of whitewashing him now seem pretty slim.

John Montagu succeeded to the earldom at the age of eleven. After Eton (where the poet Thomas Gray remembered him as a "dirty boy playing at cricket"), Cambridge, and the inevitable Grand Tour, he took up politics as a member of the Duke of Bedford's party. He first entered the Admiralty in 1744, became First Lord three years later, and was dismissed in 1751 when his party fell from favor. Twenty years afterward he was again made First Lord, and served

in that post for eleven years. This rather uninterest-
ing chronology is not historically unimportant; if
instead of the Earl of Sandwich an efficient, honorable, and dedicated man had been in charge of the
Admiralty from 1771 to 1782, the fate of the thirteen
colonies across the Atlantic might have been quite
different.

In the earl's defense it must be said that at the beginning of his political career he was a model of
industriousness, an eloquent speaker, a supporter of
reform in the dockyards. His party was in power, and
he was rising very fast within its ranks. But such are
the vagaries of English politics that suddenly, without
warning, his party was out, and his star stopped
short in its ascendancy. In the House of Commons,
when a member's party is out he sits with the Opposition and takes every opportunity to attack the party
that is in. But a peer in power or out is allowed only
to sit in the House of Lords, and the Lords can be
pretty boring. That is what happened to the Earl of
Sandwich.

During the twenty years that somebody else was
sitting in the Admiralty, Sandwich began his association with that body known variously as the Hell Fire
Club, the Order of St. Francis, or the Brotherhood
of Medmenham. In an age noted for its licentiousness, the club was notorious. Its fourteen-odd members met in an old abbey at Medmenham, ridiculed
the Catholic Church by assuming monks' habits,
drank a lot, and occasionally imported prostitutes
from London. Hearsay had it that they also held
black masses and wild orgies. Be that as it may, Sand-

wich and another of the brotherhood, John Wilkes, had a falling out, reportedly because Sandwich, in the process of invoking the devil during a black mass, was attacked by a black baboon, which Wilkes, as a joke, had appropriately equipped with horns and hoofs. Wilkes, a Member of Parliament, had become a controversial figure by publishing an antigovernment newspaper, *The North Briton,* which in its famous issue No. 45, attacked a speech by the king himself. Wilkes had been prosecuted in the Commons, which had voted No. 45 to be seditious libel and had ordered it burned by the common hangman.

Meanwhile in the Lords, Sandwich took his revenge for the baboon. Announcing that he had a grave communication to make to their Lordships, Sandwich read aloud a poem called the "Essay on Woman," a blasphemous and indecent parody of Pope's "Essay on Man," which he attributed to Wilkes, although it had actually been composed by someone else. The parody had been printed — for private circulation only — on Wilkes's printing press. Unfortunately, no copy has survived. Sandwich's intention was obviously to discredit Wilkes further, but his fellow Lords were as fascinated by the spectacle of Sandwich playing the role of guardian of public morals as they were by the actual contents of the poem. Public opinion was much aroused by the whole affair, for the people, not knowing about the baboon (if indeed it had ever existed), felt that the earl was sacrificing friendship for partisan politics. Sandwich was held in the greatest contempt for betraying his friend Wilkes. By chance *The Beggar's Opera* was then playing at Covent Garden, and when in the last scene Macheath says, "That Jemmy Twitcher should peach on me I own surprises me," the audience, applying his words to the events of the day, rose and applauded. Sandwich was known as Jemmy Twitcher from that time on.

Then there was the matter of Martha Ray. After some years of a marriage that was blessed with four children, Sandwich separated from his wife, who went to live at Windsor. The relatively young earl was unwilling to go through life alone, yet unable to divorce and remarry. So he took under his protection Martha Ray, the sixteen-year-old daughter of a stay-maker. He sent her to France to learn languages and deportment, taught her to play the harpsichord and sing, and then settled her at Hinchingbrooke to act ostensibly as his wife. It was a curious arrangement, for although Martha had a lovely voice and was the star of the musicales Sandwich often arranged for his friends, she could not, by the unwritten rules of eighteenth-century society, be introduced to the lady guests. Nevertheless, the earl and his companion lived together more or less happily for nineteen years. She bore him five children; to his credit, he educated them exactly as he had his legitimate ones. All might have continued in happy domesticity had not Martha's charms attracted a certain young man, James Hackman by name, who had been a guest at Hinchingbrooke. He fell madly in love with her and for three years tried his best to persuade her to leave Sandwich and marry him. Finally he could no longer bear living without her and resolved to commit suicide at her feet.

On the day of the tragedy, Hackman armed himself with a brace of pistols, and stalked the vicinity of the Admiralty until he saw Miss Ray leave for Covent Garden. He took up his station at the coffee house across the way, and after the opera he mingled with the crowd until Miss Ray appeared, accompanied by the singer Signora Galli and a gentleman unknown to Hackman. When the coach arrived the signora stepped into it. Then Hackman pushed forward, laid hold of Miss Ray, and at that moment, according to his later testimony, decided that they both must die. He shot her in the head, killing her instantly, then shot himself and fell in a swoon beside her, merely wounded. He was later committed to Newgate. Although Sandwich had had nothing to do with the murder, the event caused the irregularities of his private life to become generally known just when he was being charged with a number of irregularities in his public life.

These public charges were made after Sandwich took over the Admiralty for the second time in 1771. The American colonies were already in a state of unrest, and war with France loomed as a constant threat. The English fleet was not the commanding force it was made out to be; Sandwich was quite aware of this, and to his credit, he tried repeatedly to persuade an economy-minded government to give him the funds to build it up. Thus at the outbreak of the American Revolution, the deficiencies of the English navy (which proved to be an unexpected boon to the colonists) cannot be laid solely to his mismanagement. But the earl's administration of the Admiralty during those years of crisis was an open scandal. The interest of the country was invariably sacrificed to the advancement of the party, and Sandwich employed the vast patronage of his office as a convenient vehicle for bribery and political jobbery. Officials were appointed not for their professional abilities but for their votes, and the result was far-reaching corruption and inefficiency. For example, the accounts of 1780 revealed a deficit of three hundred thousand pounds of bread. Good biscuit intended for the sailors was appropriated by keepers of the stores for their hogs. Quantities of other stores—food, clothing, and so forth—were sold by Admiralty officials for their own profit. Corruption became so widespread that many officers, including Lord Howe, refused to accept a command under Sandwich, affirming that their honor was not safe.

Fortunately for the British navy, the earl's party fell from power at last, and when it was later returned, there was evidently no thought of re-establishing Sandwich in his former post. He died at the age of seventy-four, an embittered but incredibly lucky man, for now, after two centuries, his name recalls none of the infamy with which it was synonymous in his lifetime, but rather the golden sands, palm trees, and grass-skirted inhabitants of the islands that Captain Cook named after him and the unending variety of the American national lunch.

saxophone (săk′sə-fōn′) *n.* A wind instrument having a single-reed mouthpiece, a usually curved conical metal bore, and finger keys, and made in a variety of sizes.

Antoine Joseph (known as Adolphe) Sax grew up with his ten brothers and sisters in the paternal workshop in Brussels, where even as a child he worked side by side with his father making wind instruments. The bass clarinet was his particular interest, and while trying to improve its tone, he invented the saxophone, which he first thought of as a bass instrument. Only later did he realize its potential for all registers.

While still in Brussels, Sax met Berlioz, and it was no doubt the composer who persuaded him to try his luck in Paris. He arrived with thirty francs to his name, a few specimens of his instruments, and monumental determination. He established a workshop with borrowed capital and began turning out wind instruments. But in spite of such influential friends as Meyerbeer, Halévy, Donizetti, and of course Berlioz, Sax could not break into the Paris market. Men who had been supplying the opera and other orchestras for generations took a dim view of the young Belgian upstart who believed his instruments to be on a par with their own. The musicians in these orchestras, many of whom were business partners of instrument makers, were scarcely more sympathetic. Meyerbeer and Donizetti were obliged to abandon their plans to include certain of Sax's instruments in their opera scores.

Sax next invited musicians to little performances to stimulate their interest in his instruments. One such occasion was organized for February 3, 1844, at the *Salle Herz* and was to include a piece specially written by Berlioz for Sax's instruments. Featured were to be a B-flat trumpet, a cornet, an "improved bugle" (saxhorn), a clarinet, a bass clarinet, and a saxophone. The saxophone was unfortunately not quite finished when the appointed day arrived and had to be patched together with string and sealing wax. Each instrument had its moment in Berlioz's little composition—last of all the saxophone, which had never been heard publicly in Paris. Sax was so preoccupied with whether or not his instrument would hold out that he temporarily forgot the score and was forced to sustain a single note at great length and with many delicate nuances of tone until his memory returned. The audience was delighted with the display, and the saxophone solo brought great applause.

Sax's aim was to secure the monopoly of furnishing musical instruments to the French army. His friend Général de Rumigny, aide-de-camp to Louis Philippe, was an invaluable aid, and certain newspaper writers were his staunch supporters. At a special competition organized between the French military band and a band equipped with his own instruments, the latter proved clearly superior. Sax got the army trade, and immediately all horns, oboes, and bassoons disappeared from the military bands.

Monetary success was now at his fingertips, and the entries he made in various international exhibitions throughout the rest of his life seldom brought him less than the gold medal. But Sax was no man of business; he twice went bankrupt and gradually subsided into comparative obscurity.

Sequoyah

sequoia (sĭ-kwoi′ə) *n.* Any very large evergreen tree of the genus *Sequoia,* which includes the redwood and the giant sequoia.

While living in the Cherokee territory of Tennessee, young Sequoyah and his companions would argue as to whether the mysterious power of "the talking leaf" was a gift from the Great Spirit to the white man, or the white man's own discovery.

Sequoyah's companions had seen white men with books and had seen them write messages on paper. They were convinced that this form of communication was just another of those blessings that the Great Spirit had seen fit to bestow upon the white man but not upon the red. But Sequoyah strenuously maintained the opposite: that the Great Spirit had had nothing to do with it; and that the white man had himself invented "the talking leaf." It was an argument that remained fixed in his mind and continued to haunt him with its possibilities.

Sequoyah was born about 1770, most probably the son of a white trader named Nathaniel Gist. Nobody dwelt much on these matters of little significance. The important facts were that his mother was a member of the family of the Emperor Moytoy and the legendary warrior-king Oconostota; that Sequoyah was born in the Indian village of Taskigi (later Tuskegee), just five miles from the sacred town of Echota; and that he was a Cherokee. He became a craftsman in silverwork, an accomplished storyteller, and a happy participant in the Green Corn Dances, foot-races, and ball games. And, along with his entire tribe, he was illiterate.

Sequoyah's life might have continued without incident had not a hunting accident left him partially crippled. As a result he had more leisure and more opportunity to ponder the idea that the red man also might come to possess the secret of "the talking leaf." He began to wander off into the woods and spend hours there alone, avoiding everyone, playing like a child with pieces of wood or making odd little marks with one stone on another. His wife and friends offered no encouragement, or even sympathy, for they were convinced that he was either going mad or in communication with the spirits. Months became years, and lack of sympathy became ridicule and contempt. But Sequoyah was obsessed with his dream.

At first Sequoyah tried to give every word a separate character, but eventually he realized the futility of such an approach and settled on assigning a character to each sound. When his friends and neighbors talked, he no longer heard what they said but listened to the sounds, trying to separate them and trying to identify any new sound that he might theretofore have missed. What he eventually achieved was not so much an alphabet as a syllabary—eighty-six characters representing all the sounds of spoken Cherokee

—which when combined produced a written language of remarkable simplicity and effectiveness. It had taken twelve years.

There are many stories of how Sequoyah presented his "alphabet" to his doubting people and overcame their reluctance to try it. According to one legend, there was actually a great demonstration before the chiefs during which his little daughter read aloud what the chiefs had privately told him to write on a paper and thus in a single moment amazed and convinced everyone. According to another story, the alphabet was carried piecemeal from that part of the tribe still in Tennessee to the other part now in Arkansas. So beautifully simple and precise was Sequoyah's alphabet that it could be learned in a few days. Moreover, whoever learned, taught; until suddenly a most remarkable thing had happened. Within a matter of months a population that had been almost entirely illiterate suddenly became almost entirely literate! And the lame little man who had been ridiculed by his people was now respected, revered, regarded as almost superhuman and a great benefactor.

In 1828, Sequoyah was named one of a delegation of Arkansas Cherokees that went to Washington to attempt to settle with the federal government all the unfulfilled promises of all previous treaties. Sequoyah's fame preceded him, and he was the subject of much attention in the capital. Charles Bird King asked him to sit for a portrait, and many newspapermen requested interviews. Jeremiah Evarts asked him why and how he had invented the alphabet and later wrote this account of Sequoyah's answer:

> He had observed, that many things were found out by men, and known in the world, but that this knowledge escaped and was lost, for want of some way to preserve it. He had also observed white people write things on paper, and he had seen books; and he knew that what was written down remained and was not forgotten. He had attempted, therefore, to fix certain marks for sounds, and thought that if he could make certain things fast on paper, it would be like catching a wild animal and taming it.

The result of the Washington visit was that the Cherokees agreed to yet another treaty by which they exchanged their lands in Arkansas for new and more extensive ones in what is now Oklahoma. Most of the Cherokees were still clinging desperately to their ancestral territories in Tennessee and Alabama, but the Arkansas band, to which Sequoyah now belonged, once again uprooted itself and moved westward to Oklahoma. Sequoyah, now in his sixties, built himself a new cabin with his own hands, tended his little farm, and at intervals traveled up through the woods to the salt springs. There he would live for days or weeks at a time filling his kettles, tending his fires, scooping out the salt and, Thoreau-like, pausing in his work to talk to anyone who—out of curiosity to see and speak with the now-famous Cherokee philosopher—sought him out there.

But the Great Spirit did not allow Sequoyah to end his life in the tranquillity of the forest around Lee's Creek. The federal government, which had for so long coveted the Cherokees' ancestral land in Tennessee and Alabama, contracted a treaty of removal, and well-armed soldiers drove some seventeen thousand Cherokees from their homes. The long trek westward began, months of suffering ensued, and some four thousand Cherokees died before the great mass of them began to arrive in the Oklahoma territory in the spring of 1839. Problems arose immediately. The new arrivals greatly outnumbered the already established inhabitants; there were profound conflicts over the land, over the make-up of the local government, over everything. Sequoyah, foreseeing an irreparable breach, brought his influence to bear on the side of reason and necessity. At a meeting of the tribe an act of union was adopted, and the Cherokees of Alabama, Tennessee, Arkansas, and Oklahoma joined together to become the Cherokee Nation.

But even then Sequoyah could not rest. According to tradition a band of Cherokees had migrated west of the Mississippi at just about the time that Sequoyah was born. Where were they now, these lost Cherokees who did not know of his alphabet or of the new Nation? Sequoyah, now aged, set off with a party of nine horsemen and headed south. Legend has it that before he died, somewhere deep in Mexico, he did find the lost Cherokees. Not long afterward that genus of California redwoods that included the largest trees in the world was named "sequoia" after the only man in history to conceive and perfect in its entirety an alphabet or syllabary.

shrapnel (shrăp′nəl) *n.* 1. a. An antipersonnel projectile containing metal balls, fused to explode in the air above enemy troops. b. The metal balls in such a weapon. 2. Shell fragments from any high-explosive shell.

Henry Shrapnel did not fight with Wellington's army during the final defeat of Napoleon's forces on April 18, 1815, but he was well represented. Sir George Wood, who had commanded the artillery, wrote to Shrapnel from Waterloo village three days after the battle that had it not been for his shells, it was very questionable whether any effort of the British forces could have led to the recovery of the farmhouse of La Haye Sainte. "And hence," he concluded, "on this simple circumstance hinged entirely the turn of the battle."

The shrapnel shell had first been employed more than a decade before in the British attack on Surinam, and the army's response had been enthusiastic ever since. The Duke of Norfolk had testified that his troops had derived great benefit from its use and that he considered it most desirable that the invention should not be made public. In 1813 Sir Sidney Smith, concerned that the Board of Ordnance would not send him enough shells, ordered an extra two hundred of them at his own expense.

Henry Shrapnel, one of nine children, joined the army as an officer at the age of eighteen. Almost immediately he began the experiments with round shot that he was to work at in his off-hours throughout his military career. He served at Gilbraltar, in the West Indies, and with the Duke of York in Flanders, where, during the retreat from Dunkirk, his inventive mind proved a great asset to the British cause. Observing how the wheels of the gun carriages sank into the sand as the men tried to pull them to the water's edge, he suggested that the wheels be locked so that they could be skidded over the sand. He also proposed that the British set decoy fires at night away from their own troops so that the enemy would expend its ammunition on them while the British were departing.

One problem, however, continued to vex him throughout the eighty-one years of his life. Shrapnel was never able to convince the British Government that it should recompense him for the funds he had taken from his own purse to develop his invaluable shell.

Ambrose E. Burnside

sideburns (sīd′bûrnz′) *pl. n.* Growths of hair down the sides of the face in front of the ears, especially when worn with the rest of the beard shaved off.

When General Ambrose E. Burnside rode before his troops — a big, striking figure in undress uniform and fatigue cap, large buckskin gauntlets, guns swinging loosely at the hip — he looked the picture of the brave, dashing soldier. The great, bushy whiskers flanking his honest face were a kind of personal trademark and went particularly well with his bluff, hearty manner. They seemed to set him apart as somehow superb, which he was as a soldier. It was as a commanding general that he failed.

Life in the small town of Liberty, Indiana, in the mid-nineteenth century was hardly exciting, and young Burnside spent much of his time reading about the military heroes and great battles of the past. Apprenticed to a tailor at seventeen, he was simultaneously stitching away at a coat and reading Cooper's *Tactics* when his congressional representative happened by one day, questioned him about his interests, and told him that he should be at West Point. The necessary political machinery was set in motion, and Burnside realized his childhood dream by becoming a cadet at the academy. His academic record does not appear to have been much more than adequate, but he was well-known for his rendition of "The Little Black Bull" at Benny Haven's tavern and for his abilities as chef at after-hours suppers.

The war with Mexico was not yet quite over when Burnside graduated, and he was sent to join the 3rd Artillery in Mexico City. On the way down the Ohio River by boat he lost all his travel money in a game of euchre, but he managed to borrow enough to reach his destination. Soon afterward he was sent to Newport, Rhode Island, where his battery of light artillery performed splendidly for the local citizenry on the weekly "fort days." The life of a cavalry officer was never dull. Burnside was called on to charm the ladies in Newport, chase Apaches in New Mexico, and do garrison duty in St. Louis, where he saw action only when he thrashed a newspaper reporter for calling him a "military snob." Next he was sent to Texas, where his superior officer, Colonel Graham, became involved in an argument with the chief surveyor and directed Burnside to carry his side of the story to Washington. Burnside and his three escorts dodged Apache bands and killed buffaloes for food on the treacherous first leg of the journey, arriving at Fort Leavenworth, Kansas, more dead than alive. There they were put to bed and aroused every half hour by the surgeon, who required them to walk about and drink beef tea. In spite of this interruption in the journey, they reached Washington only thirty-one days after they had left Texas—almost a full month ahead of the messenger who brought the surveyor's side of the story.

Burnside's early romantic involvements were equally exciting. Having fallen in love with a bewitching Kentucky belle while at home on leave, he proposed and was accepted. The wedding day was set. But at the altar the young bride answered the crucial question with a decided "no," and could on no account be persuaded to change her mind. Fortunately, Burnside was an optimist. On his return to Newport, he met another lovely young lady at a ball, proposed, was again accepted, and this time carried the match to a successful conclusion.

At this point Burnside resigned his commission and set up a factory to manufacture an improved rifle on which he had long been working for the army. The Bristol Rifle Works was duly established but became insolvent when Burnside lost a government contract and had to sell his dress uniform, epaulettes, and sword in order to support Mrs. Burnside while he went west to look for a job. In Chicago his old West Point classmate George B. McClellan, then vice president of the Illinois Central, gave him a job as cashier in the railroad's land office. Burnside had just been promoted treasurer of the railroad when Fort Sumter was attacked, and the governor of Rhode Island called him east to take command of the First Regiment of Rhode Island Detached Militia.

For the next five years, Burnside's life was inextricably bound up with the major events of the Civil War. In Washington during the contagious excitement of that first spring, the sunset parade by the three-month volunteers who composed his militia became one of the sights of the capital, and he commanded maneuvers before members of Congress and the Cabinet, Washington belles, and occasionally Lincoln himself. In July, 1861, the "Grand Army of the Union" marched into Virginia with Burnside at the head of the second brigade, only to be routed at the first battle of Bull Run. The "Grand Army" retreated to Washington, and the war began in earnest. The three-month regiments were disbanded, and Burnside was commissioned brigadier-general of the United States Volunteers.

Early the following year, Burnside organized an expedition of twelve thousand troops to occupy key points on the coast of North Carolina. Embarking in an improvised fleet of forty-six ferryboats, canalboats, and side-wheelers, the troops encountered howling storms and high seas before reaching Roanoke Island. There they captured five forts, and took twenty-five hundred prisoners. Burnside was accordingly promoted to major-general and offered the command of the Army of the Potomac, which he repeatedly declined. He was content to head the Ninth Army Corps but evidently gravely doubted his ability to command a whole army. His friend McClellan took the post, but after the defeat at Antietam, the President sent a brigadier-general off in a blinding snowstorm to find Burnside and persuade him to change his mind. Burnside reluctantly accepted and took command the next day.

The Army of the Potomac comprised some 250,000 men and embodied the hopes of the President, the Congress, and indeed the entire North. Up to this point, it had not exactly covered itself with glory and it did not do so in the two and a half months that Burnside commanded it. He proposed to outflank Lee in Virginia by marching the army quickly along the north bank of the Rappahannock, crossing the river on pontoon bridges to take Fredricksburg, and then proceeding on to Richmond. Speed was essential, and Burnside had the army within sight of Fredricksburg in two and a half days. But the New York Engineers with the pontoons had misunderstood their orders and did not arrive for another week. Meanwhile Lee had time to occupy the heights, and when Burnside made the bold but disastrous decision to cross the river right at Fredricksburg, Lee's main force was waiting. More than nine hundred Union soldiers died, and a special truce had to be called to bury them.

Several of Burnside's subordinates secretly reported to Lincoln that the army had lost confidence in the commanding general. In January, following the so-called Mud March — in which the army marched out of its camp opposite Fredricksburg into a torrential rainstorm and had to march right back again — Burnside dismissed four of his uncooperative generals, and Lincoln, in turn, relieved Burnside of the command.

Burnside spent the rest of 1863 in command of the Department of the Ohio, which included the territory between the Ohio and Mississippi rivers. He saw no military action but had a prominent antiwar civilian arrested and tried before a military tribunal for "treasonable utterances" during a political campaign. When the Chicago *Times* defended the victim's right of freedom of speech, Burnside ordered the paper shut down and sent a detachment of cavalry and two companies of infantry to see that it was done. President Lincoln, revoking the order, cautioned him not to arrest any more civilians or shut down any more newspapers without first consulting Washington.

In April, 1864, Burnside resumed command of his old Ninth Corps, which now included a division of black troops. They faced the enemy at Petersburg, Virginia, where one of Burnside's officers suggested tunneling from the Union side to a point under the Confederate trenches. According to the plan, fused explosives would be placed under the Southern troops. After the explosion, the Ninth Corps (Burnside selected his black division) would attack through the tunnel. A regiment of Pennsylvania coal miners put in a month's hard work on the tunnel, and the plan might have succeeded had not General Meade, then commander of the Army of the Potomac, at the last minute ordered white troops rather than black to make the initial assault. The white division had no time to train, the ensuing attack was repulsed, and Burnside was once again relieved of his command.

When the war was over, Burnside returned to Rhode Island. There he served three terms as governor and two as United States Senator. His gallantry was much admired in Washington social circles, as were his "burnsides," later transposed to "sideburns" by a less reverent generation.

silhouette (sĭl′o͞o-ĕt′) *n.* A representation of
the outline of something, usually filled in with
black or another solid color.

In 1757, when Monsieur Étienne de Silhouette became controller-general, the economy of France was
in a shambles. The Seven Years' War had just begun,
and stringent economies were needed to finance it.
Silhouette started his reforms with the farmers-
general, whom he quite literally made bankrupt; he
next subjected government officials to the same taxes
that everyone else paid; finally he severely reduced
the pensions received by all courtiers, from dukes to
mistresses.

The people applauded, and Silhouette, considering
the court reformed, undertook to change the spend-
ing habits of Louis XV himself. Would it not be an
excellent idea for the king to set an example of sacrifice for his subjects? Perhaps he might begin with the
fund set aside specifically for the king's amusements?
Louis reluctantly agreed, but he seemed so morose
in the days following that the sympathetic Duc de
Choiseul, Minister of Foreign Affairs, privately offered him funds from his department's budget so
that the king might have some diversion. Louis ac-

cepted, and in time most of the courtiers found that their pensions, too, could be renewed by quiet agreements with various officials whose funds were still intact.

Budgets, moreover, are useful only when expenses are numerable. There still remained the "royal orders on the treasury," which concealed enormous expenditures, and which, since the advent of Madame de Pompadour (see *pompadour*) as the royal favorite, had more than quadrupled. The all-encompassing "royal orders" included any number of irregular, unclassified expenses such as the king's losses at cards. It was a quagmire in which a far stronger man than Silhouette would have floundered.

Defeated by the weakness of the king and the wiles of the court, Silhouette instituted new taxes. To his credit, he tried to place the major burden on the rich rather than the poor. A form of income tax was established; domestics and servants in livery, horses, carriages, and luxuries were taxed; unmarried men were penalized by having to pay a triple capitation tax. To top it all off, the controller-general levied a four-sous-per-livre sales tax on all "articles of consumption."

Silhouette suddenly found himself far and away the most unpopular man in Paris. The privileged classes were duly enraged, while the poor saw only as far as the "four sous per livre." Parliament protested vigorously; the king gave in and started granting dispensations right and left. Silhouette, desperate, suspended all government payments, thereby destroying all credit. When Silhouette left the ministry after eight months, the country's finances were in infinitely greater disorder than when he had assumed the post of controller-general.

Silhouette was publicly loaded with derision. Breeches were made "à la Silhouette"—that is, with no pockets. A new controller-general was found, but not until the old one had become forever immortalized in the popular little shadow portraits of the day, which the people scornfully associated with the incomplete career and shadowy, unsubstantial financial policies of Étienne de Silhouette.

simony (sĭm′ə-nē, sī′mə-) *n.* The buying or selling of ecclesiastical pardons, offices, or emoluments.

Simon Magus was a magician by trade. The very word "magus," meaning "astrologer," "diviner," "sorcerer," became his surname because of the extraordinary powers of bewitchment which he practiced on all and sundry in his native Samaria. Thus it was that when Philip the Deacon came preaching the new religion, Christianity, Simon was very much interested, particularly in the evidence of miraculous events of which he heard. Philip found the Samaritans ripe for conversion, and when the Apostles back in Jerusalem heard of his success, they sent Peter and John to Samaria. On their arrival, according to the account in the Book of Acts, they laid their hands on the Samaritan converts who received the Holy Spirit from them. Simon was evidently much impressed; he sensed a power beyond his own, and in his desire to possess it, offered the two Apostles money if they would share their secret with him. Peter and John, righteously indignant, refused, but the story got around, and traffic in sacred things has been known as simony ever since.

A persistent legend has it that Simon died when he disputed his powers with Peter and Paul before Nero and attempted to prove his divinity by flying from a high window up to heaven.

spoonerism (spōo′nə-rĭz′əm) *n.* An unintentional transposition of sounds in spoken language.

 "The next hymn will be 'Kinquering Congs their tatles tike,' " announced the Reverend William A. Spooner in Chapel one morning, and thus gave birth to the spoonerism. Dean and later Warden of New College, Oxford, Canon Spooner was an albino who suffered from weak eyesight and a nervous tendency to transpose initial letters or syllables while speaking. He was known to have dismissed a student with the words, "You have deliberately tasted two worms and you can leave Oxford by the town drain." The habit much endeared him to his students, who so delighted in inventing new spoonerisms in his honor that few beyond the two just recorded can be verified. Perfectly lovely apocryphal ones exist, however, such as "Let me sew you to your sheet" and "You are occupewing my pie."

tawdry (tô′drē) *adj.* Gaudy and cheap; vulgarly ornamental.

Princess Ethelreda — or Audrey, as she was later called — was the beautiful daughter of the Anglo-Saxon king Anna, who ruled East Anglia early in the seventh century, when Christianity was still new to Britain. According to the chroniclers, Ethelreda led a childhood of extraordinary piety, although she loved jewelry and would weigh herself down with strings of beads and other finery. So adorned she became, if anything, even more desirable to the eligible neighboring princes. The most ardent of these was Tombert, Prince of the Gyrwians, who asked for her hand in marriage. King Anna readily agreed, but the prospective bride resisted fiercely; she had announced her intention of following the example of the Blessed Virgin and consecrating herself wholly to God. However, the king was adamant. Given her turn of mind, Ethelreda could not have been more fortunate. Her new husband was so considerate of her feelings that when he died three years after they were married, the princess was still a virgin.

King Anna also died, and for five years the young

widow secluded herself in religious devotions, probably supposing that she was forever delivered from the threat of matrimony. But such was not the case. Egfrid, the eldest son of the great King of Northumbria and the most powerful of the Anglo-Saxon monarchs, fell in love with her. To ally themselves with the great Northumbrians was an opportunity not to be missed; or so Ethelreda's uncle, the new king, assured the reluctant young widow.

So Egfrid and Ethelreda were wed. However, Egfrid simply did not understand a wife who had pledged her virginity to God. His bride's refusals only fanned his ardor, and in desperation he appealed to his great friend Wilfrid, the Bishop of York, who since their marriage had acquired considerable influence with the new queen. But Wilfrid too had apparently fallen in love with the lovely Ethelreda, and he was much more sympathetic to her pious wishes than to her husband's plight. At the same time that he soothed the king, he secretly encouraged the queen in her resistance, even to the point of promising her heaven as a reward for her perseverance. He exacted a vow of chastity from her, then suggested that she separate from the king in order to enter a monastery. But Egfrid would not hear of it.

In such a manner twelve years passed; then the king gave up hope and consented to his wife's departure. Ethelreda immediately left for Coldingham, a monastery by the sea, which was governed by Ebba, the king's own aunt. Wilfrid followed her closely, bearing the black gown and veil that would cut her off forever from earthly husbands. Meanwhile, Egfrid had had second thoughts, and feeling himself unable to endure the sacrifice his wife had forced upon him, he set out in hot pursuit, determined to assert his rights once and for all. On Ebba's advice Ethelreda disguised herself as a poor woman and fled south, accompanied by two nuns. The three women encountered all kinds of difficulties, until finally they crossed the river that separated Northumbria from East Anglia. Ethelreda was now safe in her own land, which had been left to her by her first husband.

Here it was—on the Island of the Eels, or Ely, which was completely surrounded by fens that could only be crossed by boat—that Ethelreda built her great monastery and was joined each year by more Anglo-Saxon virgins. Wilfrid, of course, came too, remaining to make her abbess and to give the veil to her nuns. Eventually the place grew into one of the remarkable double monasteries for both men and women. Her fear for her chastity now put to rest, Ethelreda was able to concentrate on fasting and prayer; she was thought to be especially virtuous because she took hot baths only four times a year, on the vigils of the four great feasts, and then only after she had first washed the rest of her flock with her own hands. She died of the plague after seven years as abbess, leaving poor Egfrid at last free to marry again, if he still had the will.

The word "tawdry" is a corruption of "Saint Audrey" (which she was often called) and came to identify the cheap souvenirs (especially the gaudy lace neckpieces) that were hawked at her shrine and sold at Ely's annual fair.

Theodore Roosevelt

teddy bear (tĕd′ē bâr) *n.* A child's toy bear, usually stuffed with soft material and covered with furlike plush.

In the second year of his presidency, Theodore Roosevelt went down to Mississippi to hunt bears in the country around the Little Sunflower River. Anxious that the expedition be an unqualified success—that is, that the President get his bear—his hosts managed on the first day of the hunt to corner a small brown bear, which they stunned with a blow on the head and tied to a tree. But Roosevelt, always more interested in the hunt than the booty, refused to shoot it. In fact, he insisted that it be released.

The news media got hold of the story, and Clifford K. Berryman, feature cartoonist for the Washington *Post,* created "Drawing the Line in Mississippi," a cartoon that was reprinted in hundreds of publications across the country. Toy makers pounced on the idea and produced the lovable "teddy bear," which became a symbol for Roosevelt and without doubt improved his image with his electorate. It also provoked a variety of amusing situations. When in 1911 Roosevelt went to Cambridge, England, to receive a degree, he was welcomed on his arrival by a double line of students flanking his path. At the final turn in this walk, he met a teddy bear seated on the pavement with one paw outstretched in greeting. Later, as Roosevelt received his degree, a very large teddy bear was lowered onto him from the ceiling. It was, Roosevelt discovered, all part of the tradition — Darwin, in similar circumstances, had had a monkey lowered upon him.

timothy (tĭm′ə-thē) *n.* A grass, *Phleum pra-tense,* native to Eurasia, having narrow, cylindrical flower spikes, and widely cultivated for hay.

Timothy Hanson was a Maryland planter who first cultivated the grass that bears his name after having brought it from Britain to the colonies early in the eighteenth century. As he is also mentioned in connection with its cultivation in New York and the Carolinas, it is just possible that he was a kind of Johnny Appleseed of hay. Obviously, he was a friendly, neighborly man, or we would today be growing hanson instead of timothy.

victoria (vĭk-tôr′ē-ə) *n.* 1. A low, light four-wheeled carriage for two with a folding top and an elevated driver's seat in front. 2. A touring car with a folding top usually covering only the rear seat.

Young Queen Victoria's pony phaeton was low-hung to allow her to enter the carriage without having to climb several steps. By 1851, when the queen's popularity was at its peak as a result of the Crystal Palace exposition (so beautifully organized by her beloved Albert), the low-hung model of pony phaeton was already being referred to as a "victoria." That same year a Mr. Andrews of Southampton built a new victoria for the queen and delivered it to her on the Isle of Wight, where she was on holiday. Its extreme lightness and the elegance of its beautifully painted ironwork delighted the queen and her consort.

The victoria remained the queen's favorite conveyance. In winter it had of necessity to be changed for a closed vehicle such as the brougham (see *brougham*) or hansom (see *hansom*), but the inclement weather of the English summer always made the victoria preferable to the stanhope—a completely open carriage named for the Reverend Fitzroy Stanhope, an English clergyman of no other renown at all.

volt (vōlt) *n.* The International System unit of electric potential and electromotive force, equal to the difference of electric potential between two points on a conducting wire carrying a constant current of one ampere when the power dissipated between the points is one watt.

Alessandro Giuseppe Antonio Anastasio Volta was born into a family of lesser Italian nobility. He was the youngest son of a father who had been a Jesuit priest for eleven years before leaving the order to marry and raise nine children. The family was so poor that there was seldom enough money for copy books and pencils, but Alessandro was an exceptional boy. By the time he left school at sixteen, he had a command of English, French, and Latin as well as Italian; he read Dutch and Spanish fluently and had composed a classical poem of some five hundred verses on the observations and discoveries of the English chemist Joseph Priestley.

Volta was still a small child when Benjamin Franklin flew his kite in a thunderstrom, but he read about it later and became increasingly fascinated with the phenomenon of electricity. When he was twenty-four, he completed his *electrophorus*, which is still used in classrooms to demonstrate static electricity; at twenty-six he proposed and showed the practicability of an electric signal line from Como (his home) to Milan;

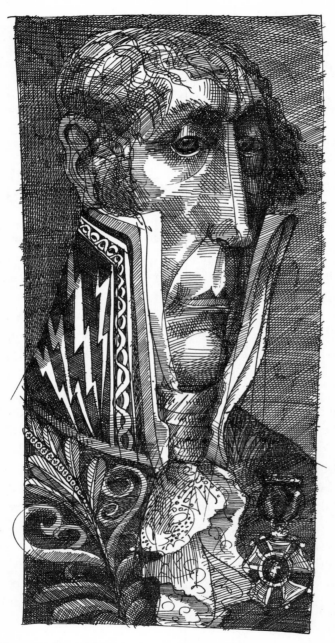

Alessandro Giuseppe Antonio Anastasio Volta

and at twenty-seven he was offered, and accepted, the professorship of physics at the University of Pavia.

Gases interested Volta; he discovered that marsh gases were inflammable and he demonstrated just how it was that gases expanded under heat. He also perfected the sensitivity of the electrometer, an instrument designed to measure the subtlest of electric charges, such as that generated by the mere evaporation of water from a basin.

Volta loved to travel for the opportunity it gave him to exchange ideas with other scientists. While in Geneva he crossed into France in order to meet Voltaire at Ferney; the eighty-year-old French philosopher drove to their rendezvous in a luxurious carriage preceded by two mounted heralds. In Paris he met the astronomer Laplace, the naturalist Count Buffon, the chemist Lavoisier, and most important, Benjamin Franklin. In England he made the acquaintance of Priestley, Sir Joseph Banks, James Watt (see *watt*), and the American potato, which he carried back to Pavia to be cultivated there.

At Pavia Volta read of Galvani's experiment with the frogs. He was interested enough to repeat it himself, only to disprove the Bologna professor's theories (see *galvanize*) and to become the focal point of the opposing school of thought, which gained adherents all over Europe. In 1791 he was elected to the Royal Society and three years later became the first foreigner ever to be awarded the Society's Copley Medal.

In his experiments with metals, Volta found that some were more easily stimulated to generate electricity than others; he drew up a list (later known as the electrochemical series) placing them in their order of effectiveness. From this he was able to formulate one of the most important laws of electrical science — that when two metals are joined, the further apart they are in the list, the more electrically effective they will prove to be. Thus it was that when he built his famous "pile," he chose plates of zinc (highest on his list) and silver (near the bottom), alternating them with moist pads, and stacking them until he had eight to ten such sandwiches. When the bottom and top of the pile were touched with a conductor, a strong electric force was produced; he had made the first battery. He wrote of his discovery to the president of the Royal Society and spent many anxious moments waiting for his letter to cross France and reach England at a time when those two countries were at war.

Soon after the publication of his discovery, the newly formed National Institute of France invited Volta to come to Paris to lecture. This he did, and remained there four months, becoming the talk of Paris by virtue of his good looks, brilliance, and charm. He gave three lectures, which Napoleon himself attended. Dressed in the robes of an academician, the First Consul personally helped Volta to decompose water into its elements by the use of electricity from his pile. His audience was enthusiastic, and Napoleon was so delighted that he made Volta a member of the institute, then a knight, and finally a count and a senator from Lombardy. Victor Hugo writes of Napoleon entering the library of the National Institute, seeing the inscription "Au Grand Voltaire" on the wall, and then crossing out the last three letters.

Volta did not marry until late in life because his intended was the youngest of the seven daughters of Count Ludovico Peregrini, and husbands for the elder six had to be found first. Some years later when Volta proposed to retire from the University of Pavia to devote himself to his sons' education, Napoleon wrote disapprovingly, "A good general ought to die on the field of honor." As Napoleon was by then Emperor of Italy as well as of France, Volta took the hint. He was rewarded when Napoleon visited his class and eulogized him before his assembled students.

God Hath Watt Wrought

James Watt

watt (wŏt) *n.* A unit of power in the International System equal to one joule per second.

James Watt was brought up on porridge and the Celtic romances of his native Scotland. His family was poor, and he seems to have had little formal education, although he developed extensive botanical and mineral collections from his summer roamings around Loch Lomond. He read widely in all the sciences and was once discovered carrying the head of a recently dead child (which he had managed to procure somewhere) into his room to dissect. At seventeen he went to Glasgow to become a mathematical instrument maker, then to London to perfect himself in the trade. He spent a miserable year in the capital; his funds were very limited, the work was hard, and his country nose was unaccustomed to the smells of the crowded eighteenth-century city. He found he could not even go out after dark for fear of being shanghaied into the navy or kidnapped and sent to the plantations.

On his return to Glasgow, Watt found a new obstruction to his career—the hammermen's guild, which included instrument makers in its membership, would not let him set up a workshop in the town. Seven years of apprenticeship were required, and no exceptions could be made for a man who had been in such a hurry that he learned the trade in one. The university came to his rescue, offering him a room within its precincts and designating him "Mathematical Instrument Maker to the College of Glasgow." With this august title, Watt, who was not yet twenty, set up shop and soon found his quarters doubling as the unofficial common room for young intellectuals — both students and professors. They spent their evenings there, not so much to relax as to find stimulation in each other's company and to hash out the latest problem in the mathematics of physical science with their young friend who — although he had never had any formal university training — was generally recognized as their superior.

Watt took his work very seriously. His chief delight was caring for the university's delicate mathematical instruments, but he also mended spectacles, made fishing rods and tackle, and repaired and tuned musical instruments. Although he claimed that he could not distinguish one note from another, he nevertheless constructed an organ that incorporated various ingenious mechanical improvements, which were much admired by local organists.

When the university's professor of natural philosophy discovered that his small model of Newcomen's steam engine, which he used in his demonstrations, had broken down, he sent it to Watt. But Watt could never simply repair a machine; he had to investigate all its parts and understand how it worked. He dismantled the little machine—a crude contraption noted more for the noise it made than for the power it transmitted—and he carefully rebuilt it. Two years later his own "improvement" was ready. His guiding principle had been to utilize all the latent heat (in this case steam), then to harness it into pushing a piston, pumping a mine, or turning a wheel. Watt's steam engine had a separate condenser—an air pump—to bring steam into the condenser, and insulation for parts of the engine. It was the first real steam engine, for the steam not only produced the vacuum but acted as the moving force as well.

Most of the rest of Watt's life was involved with his steam engine, first in producing it and then in protecting the patent against industrial pirates. More than once his plans and drawings were stolen and sold to rival companies, and spies were sent from France, Germany, and Russia to masquerade as workers and try to discover the secret of the engine. Later Watt invented a letter-copying press, a clothes dryer, a drawing machine, a machine for copying sculpture, and the word "horsepower." But by designation of the International Electrical Congress of 1895, his name survives in electricity rather than steam.

wisteria (wĭ-stîr′ē-ə) *n.* Also **wistaria** (wĭ-stâr′ē-ə). Any of several climbing woody vines of the genus *Wisteria,* having compound leaves and drooping clusters of showy purplish or white flowers.

Casper Wistar was a Philadelphia Quaker who became a professor of chemistry and physiology at the College of Philadelphia in the same year that George Washington became President. Wistar wrote the first American textbook on anatomy and was the first to describe the posterior portion of the ethmoid bone in its most perfect state; he had, however, his lighter side. His Sunday afternoon "at-homes" were famous social events in Philadelphia. He joined the American Philosophical Society and succeeded Thomas Jefferson as its president. Unlike his European colleagues Drs. Fuchs, Magnol, and Zinn (see *fuchsia, magnolia,* and *zinnia*), Dr. Wistar appears to have had little to do with botany directly. It was his good friend the Abbé Correa da Serra, the Portuguese minister to the United States, a well-known botanist and a frequent guest at Wistar's Sunday afternoons, who proposed naming the lovely climber after him.

zeppelin (zĕp′ə-lĭn) *n.* A rigid airship having a long, cylindrical body supported by internal gas cells.

Count Ferdinand von Zeppelin was bred to adventure. He was born in the mid-ninteenth century on a small island in Lake Constance that was then part of the kingdom of Württemberg. He was taught to be fearless much as most children are taught to be cautious. In the winter of his sixth year, during a mountain-climbing expedition, he crossed a narrow gorge, clinging to his father's back while his father wriggled along a girder which was all that remained of an old bridge. At ten, during the revolution of 1848, the boy acted as a courier between his father in Constance and his uncle in Switzerland. Zeppelin simply rode his pony right past the Swiss guards who patrolled the frontier. Then, like all sons of the German upper classes, he was sent to the War Academy and began his career in the army before he was twenty. But unlike his fellow cadets, Zeppelin was bored by the army and before the first year was out he petitioned the War Office to allow him to go to the University of Tübingen to study engineering. Engineering was definitely not an upper-class occu-

Count Ferdinand von Zeppelin

pation, or even a hobby, but Zeppelin could be very persuasive, and an exception was made. After a year of study he made the equally unconventional move of joining the bourgeois officers of the Engineer Corps.

But four years of peacetime with the Engineer Corps left him longing for excitement, and when the American Civil War broke out, Zeppelin petitioned the King of Württemberg for leave to go. Officially he was to study the organization of a militia army but actually he sought adventure and a chance to see the world. He must have traveled with considerable baggage, for on the cruise from New York down to Baltimore he was able to supply the officers with enough Rhine wine for them to party through the night. At dawn he climbed to the top of the mast to prove that he was still sober. He was bound for the Union army, carrying a letter of introduction to President Lincoln in one pocket, and in another— just in case he should be captured by the Confederates—one to Robert E. Lee. When the young count, dressed in morning coat and top hat, arrived at the White House for an interview, he was greeted by a rather shaggy and unkempt Lincoln and his private secretary, Reed, who, as Zeppelin later recorded in his diary, "sat down on the desk during the short interview and dangled his feet which hung loosely from his trousers and which were clothed in moccasins."

Zeppelin then attached himself to General Hooker's Army of the Potomac and took part in several battles before he joined an expedition that set out to search for the source of the Mississippi River in the Montana Rockies. Two Russians and two Indians made up the balance of the party, but no one was experienced in wilderness exploration. They lost their trail and wandered aimlessly about for days, existing on water rats and almost dying of thirst before they reached civilization again. The most important moment in the trip as far as Zeppelin was concerned was a stop-over in St. Paul, Minnesota, on the way back to the war. There he made his first balloon ascent, and there this Prussian army officer, looking down at the little midwestern American river town, first conceived the idea of the dirigible—a structure that could be filled with gas like a balloon, could rise into the air like a balloon, and yet could be navigated like a ship.

On his return to the Union army, Zeppelin attached himself to the balloon staff. McClellan's army had two balloons, which were used for observation and which required four horses to transport them. The Confederate army had only one balloon, a very beautiful, multi-colored one, made entirely of silk dresses that Southern ladies had sacrificed to the cause. Zeppelin took part in several battles, including Fredricksburg (where he no doubt met General Burnside—see *sideburns*), before the outbreak of hostilities between Prussia and Austria called him back to Europe.

The war of 1866 proved all too brief. As adjutant to King Charles I of Württemberg, Zeppelin saw far too little action to suit him. His sole exploit was swimming fully clothed and booted across the swollen Main River to deliver an important message to the

Hessian troops on the opposite bank. The Franco-Prussian war of 1870 was more to his liking. Only a few hours after the two countries had declared war, Zeppelin led a reconnaissance expedition into French territory to determine the extent of French mobilization. His tactic was to ride through the towns with his small party so fast that everyone would be too surprised to attempt to stop them. At Trimbach, however, he paused long enough to tear down Napoleon III's proclamation from the door of the Town Hall and lost his horse to pursuing lancers. Near Gundershofen the group halted for a quick meal and were surrounded by French *chasseurs à cheval;* all but Zeppelin were killed. When two days later he finally made his way back to the Bavarian frontier with his information, he was much praised for his daring. What most impressed him about the war, however, was not his own bravery, but an event he viewed from staff headquarters during the siege of Paris—the spectacular escape from the capital of the gallant Frenchman Leon Gambetta by balloon.

Soon after the war Zeppelin began to draft the first plans for his dirigible ship—plans that he kept secret for the next fifteen years. Finally, shortly before his fiftieth birthday, he wrote a report to the King of Württemberg on what he considered to be requirements of military airships. He wrote that they must be able to navigate against strong air currents and remain in the air for at least twenty-four hours at a time, and that they must be able to carry aloft a considerable number of men, supplies, and ammunition. The problems that remained to be resolved, he concluded, were the most efficient shape for the craft, how it might be made to rise without throwing off ballast, and how it might be made to descend without letting out—and thus wasting—great quantities of air.

After a brief stint as Württemberg's ambassador plenipotentiary to Prussia, Zeppelin was suddenly retired from the army by Kaiser William II of Prussia for being too independent. Not at all at a loss, the count began the first of what was to become a long series of experiments on Lake Constance. All summer long he and his faithful assistant Theodore Kober could be spotted in the middle of the lake in their little boat with its huge propeller. His neighbors began to call him the crazy count, but three years later plans for *Luftschiff Zeppelin 1* were complete.

Zeppelin soon discovered, however, that inventing was the least of his worries. A commission of scientific experts declared his airship too impractical to consider seriously, and the Prussian Ministry of War would not even grant him a patent. Too patriotic to seek a patent elsewhere, Zeppelin waited for two more years until the press became interested and sponsored a public subscription. With money finally available, a pontoon hangar was built in Lake Constance and construction of the airship began.

Luftschiff Zeppelin 1 made its first flight in the summer of 1900, with the count, now sixty-two, at the helm. Thousands trooped to the shores of the lake to watch, almost reverently, as the airship rose to 1,300 feet, traveled some three and a half miles through the air, and landed safely exactly seventeen minutes later. The people were delighted, but seventeen minutes in the air did not convince the government, which decided against investing. With the funds exhausted, the airship and its hangar were dismantled.

But once again events on the other side of the Atlantic intervened in Zeppelin's life. There was to be a great fair in St. Louis, and why should not all the world witness that miracle of modern German scientific invention, the dirigible? Another subscription was begun, a state lottery was instituted, and Zeppelin in his eagerness contributed what was left of his own private fortune. The pontoon hangar was rebuilt, and *Luftschiff Zeppelin 2* was begun.

Unfortunately, *LZ 2* never made it to St. Louis. On its first flight, it developed engine trouble, its steering failed, and although Zeppelin managed to land it safely in a field, a storm destroyed it that very night. The King of Württemberg was by now, however, completely sold—he simply floated another state lottery, and *Luftschiff Zeppelin 3* was begun. *LZ 3* had two wing-shaped surfaces jutting from its sides, and it was an instant success. Officials of the Prussian government, realizing that the airship was evidently going to succeed irrespective of their approval and aid, decided to get on the bandwagon. A German national lottery was instituted, and the Reichstag passed a bill granting subsidies for airship construction. A huge new hangar on Lake Constance was begun, and the *luftschiff* came officially into fashion. Flights of *LZ 3* resumed; local accommodations for important spectators became a matter of concern, and construction of *LZ 4* began.

The Reichstag was more interested in military than scientific accomplishments, however, so *LZ 4* was constructed with a platform on top for a machine gun. On its fourth flight which lasted an unprecedented twelve hours, it cruised over Switzerland at the unheard of speed of forty miles per hour. The people's excitement knew no bounds. "The Zeppelin is coming!" was the cry that went up from one Swiss hamlet after another, accompanied by rousing cheers for the calm, white-haired man sailing above them. Zeppelin suddenly found himself a national hero; his seventieth birthday was celebrated for days by delegations, speeches, songfests, fireworks, and of course the inevitable honorary degrees.

LZ 4 completed a twenty-four-hour flight and then went up in flames during an electrical storm. Several lives were lost in the incident, and Zeppelin, very shaken, spoke of retiring. But the public would not hear of it. Over six million marks were subscribed to build *Luftschiff Zeppelin 5*. In fact, the general feeling was that a whole fleet of airships must be built. So Zeppelin gave up thoughts of retirement and founded the new Airship Construction Works Zeppelin. At the helm of *LZ 5* he flew to Berlin, where he was welcomed and decorated by the same kaiser who had sacked him from the military twenty years previously.

Zeppelin was seventy-six when World War I began and he died before the German defeat was quite certain. During the war, eighty-eight airships were built and equipped with bomb racks and a bombing station. Air raids were actually made over Paris and London, but in combat the dirigible proved slow and unwieldy compared to the airplane, and few of the eighty-eight were intact when the war ended. As for the old count, he applied in vain to be sent to the front with his old regiment; he had to be content with celebrating his last Christmas with them in trenches that remained quiet because of the day's truce.

zinnia (zĭn′ē-ə) *n*. Any of various plants of the genus *Zinnia,* native to tropical America; especially, *Z. elegans,* widely cultivated for its showy, variously colored flowers.

It is commonly believed that the name of a plant which is derived from that of a botanist shows no connection between the two," wrote Linnaeus. "But anyone who has but slight knowledge of the history of letters will easily discover a link by which to connect the name with the plant, and indeed there will be such charm in the association that it will never fade from his memory." Johann Gottfried Zinn, a famous German botanist of the mid-eighteenth century, rose to the position of professor at Göttingen before he died at the age of thirty-two. Like his lovely namesake, he bloomed brightly and abundantly and with great promise but fell with the first frost.